"Cavaiola and Lavender have done it again! They have given us another perfect combination of psychological science and real-life applications to provide a highly readable guide to living and working with people who drive us crazy. Alive with examples and suggestions, this book is not only perfect for counselors and therapists, but also for anyone who deals with controlling perfectionists at home or on the job."

—Richard Ponton, PhD, associate professor at Georgian Court University in Lakewood, New Jersey

*Impossible to Please* is a candid, informative, and thought-provoking study of the controlling perfectionist. Lavender and Cavaiola illuminate our understanding of obsessive-compulsive personality disorder while providing suggested actions for dealing effectively with these individuals at home, at work, and in the community."

—Suzanne D. Mudge, PhD, associate professor and program coordinator of counseling and guidance at Texas A&M University

"After being in managerial and leadership positions for over 40 years, I wish I could say that I never had to deal with a perfectionist personality. Unfortunately, that is not the case. I have had experiences with toxic coworkers and, to say the least, they were indeed troublesome. Drs. Lavender and Cavaiola's first book, *Toxic Coworkers*, was of great help during these trying times. Like their other books, *Impossible to Please* is filled with wisdom and insights into this challenging area. I strongly recommend this most practical and applicable book."

—Louis A. Scheidt, PE, PP, president and CEO of Innovative Engineering, Inc.

# Impossible *to* Please

## How to Deal *with* Perfectionist Coworkers, Controlling Spouses, *and* Other Incredibly Critical People

NEIL J. LAVENDER, PhD
ALAN A. CAVAIOLA, PhD

New Harbinger Publications, Inc.

## Publisher's Note

Distributed in Canada by Raincoast Books

Copyright © 2012 by Neil J. Lavender & Alan Cavaiola
New Harbinger Publications, Inc.
5674 Shattuck Avenue
Oakland, CA 94609
www.newharbinger.com

All Rights Reserved

Acquired by Jess O'Brien; Cover design by Amy Shoup;
Edited by Will DeRooy; Text design by Michele Kermes

Library of Congress Cataloging-in-Publication Data

Lavender, Neil J.
    Impossible to please : how to deal with perfectionist coworkers, controlling spouses, and other incredibly critical people / Neil J. Lavender and Alan Cavaiola.
        p. cm.
    Includes bibliographical references.
    ISBN 978-1-60882-348-2 (pbk. : alk. paper) -- ISBN 978-1-60882-349-9 (pdf e-book) -- ISBN 978-1-60882-350-5 (epub)
    1. Criticism, Personal. 2. Perfectionism (Personality trait) 3. Interpersonal conflict. 4. Interpersonal relations. I. Cavaiola, Alan A. II. Title.
    BF637.C74L38 2012
    158.2--dc23
                                2012021943

Printed in the United States of America

15  14  13          10 9 8 7 6 5 4 3 2

# Contents

# Acknowledgments

First, we acknowledge and give thanks to our families for putting up with us while we wrote this book. You've always given us the space and encouragement we need to take on such tasks as research and writing.

We also thank our patients and our students. You're by far some of the finest people we've ever met. We applaud your courage and motivation and your hunger for the truth and personal growth. You've achieved so much while overcoming so many obstacles. We're so fortunate to be working in the field that we love, and you're such a big part of this. You challenge us every day to know and do more. Hopefully, in our teaching and therapy, we've been able to challenge you to overcome difficult hurdles in your lives, thereby enriching your lives in some way.

Our thanks wouldn't be complete without acknowledging the plentiful support we received from all the staff at New Harbinger. This is our third book with you, and you've never failed in your professionalism and guidance. Special thanks to acquisitions editor Jess O'Brien. Thanks also to editorial manager Jess Beebe and associate editor Nicola Skidmore for taking us through this process step by step. Dr. Matt McKay and Angela Autry Gorden, whose recommendations helped shape the direction of this book: we couldn't have done this without your wisdom and expertise. To Will DeRooy of Intelligent Editing, a special shout out for the final edits—your suggestions were right on the mark.

# Introduction

You picked up this book most likely because you're struggling in a relationship in which you feel the other person perceives you as not good enough. Perhaps this person is your spouse, or perhaps it's your parent, a coworker, or your boss. In any event, this person seems to habitually criticize you. What you do never seems good enough for this person—in everything you undertake, you constantly fall short of some perfect standard. If you're like most of the people with this problem we've encountered over the years, you experience numerous and often conflicting emotions in this relationship. You might feel sad or angry or even inadequate. Most likely you feel confused. You may have tried all you can to make this person happy, only to fail again and again.

> Marianne was a grade school teacher who for eleven years received excellent evaluations from all of her supervisors. She got along well with her fellow teachers and staff and was twice voted teacher of the year. Parents often approached Marianne after the school year was over, thanking her personally for their students' progress.
>
> But when Marianne's principal was replaced by a woman who promised "a more hands-on approach," it seemed that Marianne could do nothing right. Although she followed the new principal's every recommendation, she received a poor performance evaluation, and when she tried to defend herself and provide explanations in response, the principal only dug her heels in deeper and accused her of insubordination. Letters and e-mails flew back and forth until one day the principal presented Marianne with a

*notice of termination containing many rather vague reasons, the most puzzling of which was "a poor attitude."*

*Marianne was stunned.* How could this have happened? *she thought. I did everything right. I'm a great teacher. How is it I could never be good enough for her?*

*Francine met Marco while she was still in high school. She always told her girlfriends, "I fell in love with him because he's the best at everything." He was a straight "A" student, the star of his basketball team, and the president of the student council. He was well mannered, hard working, and respectful of all in authority.*

*But soon after Francine and Marco were married, he became emotionally distant, more involved with his work than he was with her and, eventually, the children. Whenever she became romantic, he claimed she was being childish. When she asked him to contribute to the household expenses, he'd reply that he couldn't because she'd just "spend it frivolously." But worst of all, he subjected her to a barrage of constant criticism: he didn't like her friends, her family get-togethers ("They're all just a sideshow of scatterbrained chatter"), her laugh, her lovemaking, her housekeeping, her grammar. He even criticized her for the way she put the magazines in the magazine rack, claiming that the covers should be all be facing out and that she should know that was "the only way magazines should ever be put away." He lectured her constantly on how she needed to make changes in her life.*

*Finally, at the end of her rope, and crying herself to sleep every night in abject loneliness, Francine began to consider consulting with a divorce attorney.*

Perhaps the saddest example of a person with this problem is a child who's never good enough in a parent's eyes. At least adults can escape a situation in which they feel that they're never good enough, but children can't. Such a child may bring home a score of 95 on an essay and be criticized for not getting 100. The child who helps her parents for two hours may be criticized for not helping for three hours. The child who scores a touchdown may be criticized for not winning the game. Second place is never good enough. These children's bedrooms can never be clean enough; their friends can never be smart enough or nice enough. Feeling helpless and needing their parents' love and protection, these children are forced into accepting the destructive idea that they're defective in some way.

Time and time again, our clients bring these types of problems to us in the hope that we can help them repair their shattered self-esteem, as well as give them new strategies for dealing with the hypercritical people in their lives. In our early careers, these problems were particularly challenging, because the cognitive behavioral therapy in which we'd been trained didn't seem to help. In other words, the plans we devised with our clients to help them deal with these difficulties seemed excellent and should have worked but for some reason didn't. Our clients were not at fault; these approaches just didn't work when people were dealing with the type of personality we discuss in this book.

As time went on, we discovered that the very same people who make those around them feel not good enough are, ironically, defective in their capacities for intimacy and normal relationships. Because they're very critical of others, they're next to incapable of having normal relationships. In other words, our clients were dealing with people who appeared to be psychologically healthy but had significant impairment, in the form of a *personality disorder.*

"Personality disorder" refers to a unique group of psychological problems in which personality traits create significant and potentially lifelong impediments to normal and healthy relationships, especially close relationships. Complicating matters is the fact that people with a personality disorder are almost always unaware that they have a problem. Amazingly enough, they perceive their inadequacies as strengths, which causes them to rarely seek help of any kind, especially psychotherapy, making it unlikely that they'll ever receive the treatment they require. They blame others for their relationship problems and go on to repeat their mistakes, the dramatic irony being that it's their wounded victims who go for help.

This book represents our third journey into the subject of personality disorders. In our first book, *Toxic Coworkers* (2000), we offered methods of dealing with people with personality disorders in the workplace. In *The One-Way Relationship Workbook* (2011), we focused specifically on narcissistic personality disorder (NPD) and its variants. Through these efforts, we were able to help thousands of people around the world navigate these stormiest of relationships.

Now we focus on hypercritical people like Marianne's principal and Francine's husband—people with obsessive-compulsive personality disorder (OCPD), whom we call *controlling perfectionists*. Such impaired individuals are all too common in our culture. While narcissists suck the very life out of those around them by using them, by exploiting them, or by forcing them to be an audience for their seemingly never-ending tales of conquest and brilliance, controlling perfectionists wear those around them down little by little by niggling, carping, and criticizing almost everything they do and making them feel that they're never good enough.

Oddly enough, these people appear to be the very embodiment of contradiction: They may be highly energetic and productive or, conversely, obstructionistic and procrastinating. They may be masters of organization and prioritization or slaves of minutiae and the irrelevant. They may appear overconfident, while at the same time their insides churn with doubt and self-deprecations. For that reason they're intriguing and often enigmatic. But almost always, in close relationships, they're cold, distant, controlling, and critical.

The more positive qualities they possess can be highly rewarded in a culture like ours that honors and rewards those who are highly productive, well organized and punctual, tidy and moral, savers rather than spenders; those who sweat even the smallest of details and who will stay up all night to make sure a project is done correctly and handed in on time. But what brings controlling perfectionists success may bring suffering to those around them. Demanding adherence to strict standards may be part of a winning strategy when coaching a basketball team, for example, but it is hardly a formula for a good marriage. And while self-criticism might drive controlling perfectionists to perform better, if they aim the same fanatical criticism at their children it may do some serious damage and contribute to the formation of emotional problems in their children. In fact, parental criticism and an invalidating environment seem to be implicated as a causal factor in many people with personality disorders (e.g., Linehan 1993).

Worse yet, you can't convince controlling perfectionists they have a problem: Tell them they're too fussy and they'll say that you're too lax; tell them they're too demanding and they'll say that you're not demanding enough. And if you tell them they're too critical, they'll simply say that they're doing you a favor by correcting you so that you won't make the same mistake again. And then they'll criticize you again for not thanking them.

As you read this book you may be surprised or even shocked to find out some facts about controlling perfectionists—and ways to handle them—that seem to contradict common sense. You'll begin to see their perfectionistic and controlling nature for the dysfunction it really is: a quality within the criticizer, not the person being criticized. Believe it or not, your relationship with a controlling perfectionist will improve once you stop trying so hard to please this person. You'll feel more confident and more empowered. You can then reduce this person's negative impact on your life and your self-esteem by setting limits and boundaries and establishing better communication.

# Outline of the Book

In part I, you'll learn to recognize the various signs of controlling perfectionism and understand the symptoms. Chapter 1 covers the particular qualities of controlling perfectionists, as well as the different subtypes. In chapter 2, we discuss controlling perfectionists in romantic, parental, and work relationships and the unique problems they present in these different settings. In chapter 3, we delineate the ways in which controlling perfectionists can get under your skin and affect you in ways that other people don't.

In part II of the book, we focus on practical strategies, because you'll find it helpful to treat a controlling perfectionist differently than you do others. In chapter 4, you'll learn the aspects of your situation that are relatively unchangeable and distinguish them from the things that you can change, thereby making your efforts more fruitful. In chapter 5, the discussion turns to how to set realistic boundaries so as to limit the detrimental effect a controlling perfectionist can have on you. Chapter 6 focuses on how to communicate more effectively and guide your interactions with a controlling perfectionist. In chapter 7, we focus specifically on effective strategies to use in friendships, in family life, and in romantic relationships, while we devote chapter 8 to the quite different topic of controlling perfectionists in the workplace. The book closes with a chapter on how to seek professional help for both yourself and the controlling perfectionist in your life, should that become necessary.

Most likely, you'll find that the entire book contains information that can be helpful whether you live with, work with, or have a friendship or other relationship with a controlling perfectionist, but you'll want to focus on the information, descriptions, and strategies that specifically pertain to your situation. So, for example, if you're dating a controlling perfectionist, you'll benefit by reading the entire book, but you should concentrate on areas describing controlling perfectionists in romantic relationships. After you've read the book, you may find it an excellent resource to consult frequently as you continue to transform your relationship.

# PART I

# Understanding Controlling Perfectionists

# CHAPTER 1

............................................

# Controlling Perfectionism
# Explained

There's a saying that perfectionists are never happy, because things are rarely, if ever, perfect. Even so, many people still constantly seek perfection. This book is not about *all* perfectionists, however; it's about the kind who not only drive themselves toward unrealistic goals but also drive others toward those goals: the control freaks, micromanagers, demanding (or even abusive) partners, helicopter parents, and workaholics. If you have such a person for a teacher, a supervisor, a romantic partner, a family member, or a coworker, you may often have a nagging feeling that you're never good enough. A controlling perfectionist is someone like Brad or Ava.

*Brad was in his fourth year of medical school when he met Susan, a nurse on the surgical unit at the medical center where he was doing one of his clinical rotations. For Susan it was love at first sight, and they began dating. Brad graduated at the top of his class in medical school and went on to specialize in neurosurgery.*

*As their relationship developed, Brad became more and more critical of Susan. He made derogatory comments about her friends and even her family. Although Susan encouraged Brad to seek therapy when his critical nature began to affect their relationship, their ability to have friends, their ability to share interests together, and his ability to work with others, he refused: he had*

*disdain for the field of mental health care and saw seeking*
*psychological help as admitting to weakness.*
    *Brad's criticism of Susan became so bad that she decided*
*to separate four years into their relationship.*

*Ava is considered one of the up-and-coming executives in the*
*corporation where she has been working for the past three years.*
*The team she manages is considered one of the best; however, the*
*senior vice president to whom Ava reports has expressed concern*
*because of the high turnover rate in Ava's department. Although*
*Ava has concluded that those who end up leaving the department*
*do so to take better jobs with better pay, ask anyone who knows*
*Ava and they'll tell you the real story. Ava is a control freak—a*
*micromanager—and eventually people on her team end up feeling*
*worthless and denigrated. What's interesting is that Ava views*
*herself as a very moral person who puts in a lot of hours and*
*expects the same from her employees. Although her friends accuse*
*her of being a workaholic, Ava feels proud that she has a position*
*of power that pays well. Ava does admit that she wishes she were*
*in a romantic relationship, but she rationalizes that she just doesn't*
*have time to date right now.*

# Definition

Interestingly, most Americans tend to consider someone who strives to be perfect or someone who aspires to be orderly and organized in very positive terms. We all can see traits in both Brad and Ava that are indeed admirable. They both are at the top of their game, work hard, and set high standards for themselves but drive others around them to work hard also. What's wrong with that, right? If you were to speak with Brad and Ava, they'd probably tell you that they're proud of what they've accomplished, yet they'd probably also tell you that they must keep up the pace and level of productivity. They're certainly proud of their organizational abilities, their orderliness, and their devotion to work. They drive themselves hard, so is there anything wrong with expecting nothing less from those around them?

In order to answer this question, we have to look beyond the positive trait to the extreme to which it's taken. For example, you'd probably agree that self-esteem or self-confidence is a healthy personality trait; however, if we exaggerate this trait to a point where a person becomes grandiose, egocentric, or narcissistic, then we're dealing with something entirely different. So too with perfectionism and control. It's one thing to direct your own life, but quite another to try to control everyone around you or demand that everyone march to your tune. This is where controlling perfectionists step over the line.

## EXERCISE: Identifying the Controlling Perfectionist

How do you spot a controlling perfectionist? The following list describes traits that controlling perfectionists commonly possess. Many of these relate to specific kinds of controlling perfectionists, which we'll discuss shortly. Thus most controlling perfectionists have some but not all of these characteristics. Think of the hypercritical person in your life and place a check mark next to the traits that you perceive this person has.

_____ 1. A need for perfection so great that it interferes with their ability to attain happiness or satisfaction in life

_____ 2. A preoccupation with rules, lists, organization, and orderliness, to such an extent that they often seem to miss the point of an activity or task

_____ 3. A tendency to procrastinate, out of a fear of not doing things right

_____ 4. A need to control the finances, schedules, and other details of the lives of those with whom they're close; moodiness and anxiety when they're not in charge

_____ 5. Unrealistically high expectations and standards for others' performance and behavior

_____ 6. An excessive devotion to work and productivity, to the point at which they have difficulty having fun or devoting time to friendships

_____ 7. An inflexibility that communicates that _their_ way is the only way

_____ 8. Stinginess with time or money; miserliness

_____ 9. A reluctance to delegate tasks to others; an attitude of "If you want something done right, do it yourself"

_____ 10. Difficulty letting go of material possessions

_____ 11. An overly conscientious or moralistic view of the world, with rigid ideas about right and wrong

_____ 12. Difficulty both expressing feelings and identifying others' feelings, as if cut off from emotional life; a cold and cheerless exterior

Chances are you checked four or more items, which indicates that you're probably dealing with a controlling perfectionist. Not all controlling perfectionists are alike, however. Below we discuss some common configurations of perfectionistic and controlling traits.

## Variations and Subtypes of Controlling Perfectionists

Theodore Millon has written extensively on various types of personality disorders and describes the controlling perfectionist as the "compulsive personality" or the "obsessive-compulsive personality." In this book we use the term "controlling perfectionist" to avoid any confusion with obsessive-compulsive disorder (OCD), which is quite different from obsessive-compulsive *personality* disorder (OCPD). Whereas OCD is characterized by obsessive thoughts of some imagined danger or by compulsively engaging in rituals, such as handwashing, counting, or checking to make sure the door is locked or the stove is turned off, OCPD relates to a need to control others and is characterized by such personality traits as rigidity, stubbornness, and a need to have everything your way or to prove others wrong.

Millon and colleagues (2004) have outlined five subtypes of the compulsive personality.

## *The Conscientious Compulsive*

Conscientious compulsives compensate for feelings of inadequacy and anxiety about their performance by rigidly adhering to the rules or desires of those in authority or power or to the rules of society. Usually described as hardworking and thorough, they're very tightly controlled people who lack spontaneity and creativity; they depend on routine, structure, rules, and regulations. They make good followers but rarely become leaders. However, when they do rise to management-level positions, their controlling tendencies become very evident. Conscientious compulsives tend to make others miserable by expecting them to be just as nitpicky. If you don't adhere to their standards, they'll become hypercritical. Negative or derogatory comments, looks of disapproval, and judgmental glances are means by which conscientious compulsives control the behavior of those around them.

Because conscientious compulsives are considerate and cooperative, especially toward those in authority, they expect to be treated the same way (whether in work or love relationships). Any perceived lack of reciprocal consideration or cooperation is likely to cause the conscientious compulsive to feel angry, abandoned, or self-deprecating. If you checked off items 2, 11, and 12 in the exercise above, chances are you're dealing with a conscientious compulsive.

## The Puritanical Compulsive

Puritanical compulsives defend against their own urges to rebel or defy authority by adopting a moral righteousness and a rigid adherence to what they consider the dictates of moral behavior. A façade of propriety or moralistic superiority masks ambivalence and resentment toward rules and authority regarding what constitutes acceptable behavior. Not surprisingly, puritanical compulsives are often attracted to religious fundamentalism, in which very strict dictates for behavior help them repress or sublimate their urges. However, puritanical compulsives can be found in just about any corporation, government agency, or societal institution, where they're often admired for the strength of their convictions yet those who truly come to know them see them as abrasive, irritating, and prudish. Puritanical compulsives are very judgmental and may view others as lazy, shiftless, or morally inferior. If you checked off items 5, 6, and 11 in the exercise above, chances are you're dealing with a puritanical compulsive.

## The Bureaucratic Compulsive

Bureaucratic compulsives overly identify with their role or job. They ally themselves with the organization, corporation, or institution for which they work so much that they seem to *become* that organization, corporation, or institution (for example, law enforcement; an educational institution, such as a university; the military; or a government agency, such as the IRS). They rigidly adhere to their employer's policies, regulations, and rules, and they expect others to do exactly the same. They often cause misery by micromanaging the lives of people around them. It's not unusual for bureaucratic compulsives to lose sight of the mission or goal—the big picture—because they get lost in the minutiae of policies and procedures. Bureaucratic compulsives may be very ingratiating and conciliatory toward their superiors yet quite vitriolic and demeaning toward their subordinates. If you checked off items 2, 4, 6, 7, and 9, chances are you're dealing with a bureaucratic compulsive.

## The Parsimonious Compulsive

Parsimonious compulsives are motivated to protect what's theirs at all costs. They're most noted for their stingy, miserly, and selfish attitude. When it comes to giving of their time, money, or possessions, they can always make some excuse not to. They may be self-sufficient to a fault and viciously guard against anyone who may deprive them of their resources or possessions, acting as if these things are irreplaceable. If you checked off items 8 and 10, chances are you're dealing with a parsimonious compulsive.

## The Bedeviled Compulsive

Bedeviled compulsives struggle with a need to oppose and sabotage, which they counter with a tendency toward inaction. By vacillating and dragging their feet when it comes to making decisions— behind a façade of self-control—they come to be seen as negativistic procrastinators who keep others from getting things done or accomplished. While they make a show of wanting to conform to others' wishes and agenda, they may give endless rationales for why they delay in making decisions or completing projects. To others, they may appear to be tightly wrapped and highly disciplined; therefore, they tend to see themselves as superior. Bedeviled compulsives can be very rigid, moralistic, and judgmental. If you checked off items 1 and 3, chances are you're dealing with a bedeviled compulsive.

## *Ebenezer Scrooge*

When Charles Dickens wrote the novella *A Christmas Carol* in 1843, little did he know that he'd be creating, in the character of Ebenezer Scrooge, the modern literary archetype of the obsessive compulsive personality disorder. Prior to his epiphany on Christmas Eve, Scrooge, the meticulous accountant, is a shining example of a controlling perfectionist. In addition to his hallmark miserliness, we also see evidence of rigid adherence to rules (when he chides Bob Cratchit for watching the clock or for having the audacity to want Christmas Day off to spend with his family). He also has difficulty expressing any warmth toward his family—his nephew and his nephew's fiancée. He abusively criticizes his colleagues and shows little sympathy for others, especially the poor. Is it easy to identify which subtype of controlling perfectionist Scrooge is?

## *Other Subtypes*

There are other controlling perfectionists you may come across in your daily life who are deserving of mention.

**The power elite.** Have you ever noticed how some extremely wealthy people feel that they've been anointed with the task of passing judgment on what's right and proper? They become extremely rigid in their perspective of what's moral or ethical, with little concern for those less fortunate. Naturally, wealth alone doesn't cause someone to become a controlling perfectionist. Although this subtype usually comes from the upper class of society, having been born with the proverbial silver spoon in their mouths and educated at elite prep schools and Ivy League universities, what sets them apart is their judgmental nature and need to control others. They tend to treat everyone as their subordinates, like servants to be controlled and bossed around.

**Religious zealots.** It's important not to confuse this subtype with truly religious and spiritual people. This subtype is characterized by people so rigid in their religious beliefs that they seem to lose compassion for others. Instead they're judgmental and manifest disdain or disgust for anyone who doesn't share their rigid moralistic views. Therefore the need to control others and to browbeat them into their way of thinking becomes paramount to their character. Instead of a "live and let live" philosophy, they adopt an opposite style: either you share their beliefs or you're judged and condemned. Although this subtype shares many commonalities with the puritanical compulsive described above, these are people who go well beyond the puritanical subtype in their wish to persecute and punish. Think of this subtype as the puritanical compulsive on steroids. If a puritanical compulsive is a very vocal judge, a religious zealot is judge, jury, and executioner. Religious zealots are capable of taking drastic action in support of their views.

**Professionally bound controlling perfectionists.** It should be no surprise that controlling perfectionists are attracted to particular occupations in which they can exert control over others. Although similar to the bureaucratic compulsive, the main distinction is that bureaucratic compulsives ally themselves with a corporation or institution, whereas professionally bound controlling perfectionists ally themselves with their profession and the power they derive from that profession. It appears that as they develop their professional identities they become more rigid and controlling. We're not saying that all accountants, attorneys, doctors, administrators, and techies are controlling perfectionists; however, it's not unusual to find perfectionists overrepresented in occupations in which precision, adherence to rules or regulations, and attention to detail are essential. We all want our doctors to be thorough and to pay attention to details, right? We don't want surgeons to leave sponges in people they operate on. Yet it's when these traits carry over to their personal lives or their relationships with family and friends (as well as their patients) that problems develop. We talk more about this subtype in chapter 8.

By now you should have a sense of just how pervasive controlling perfectionists (or "compulsive personalities") are in our society and how disruptive they can be in the workplace, in romantic relationships, in families, and in other settings. What's so unique to people with this type of personality disorder is how normal or acceptable their behavior can seem to others—normal, that is, until you go beneath the surface. After all, our society values hard work, dedication to job and family, living by the rules, and being considerate and cooperative. Yet when personal traits related to these values go to extremes, they risk causing dysfunction both interpersonally and occupationally. Because no two controlling perfectionists are alike, it's important to consider the middle ground that exists between normal and disordered behavior.

| Disordered trait | Characteristic trait | Normal trait |
| --- | --- | --- |
| Is preoccupied with lists, rules, etc., which interfere with task completion | Takes special pride in doing things right | Accomplishes tasks with little fuss or fanfare |
| Follows a dogmatic, rigid approach | Is more comfortable adhering to rules | Is flexible and able to view issues from many perspectives |
| Micromanages others; is unable to delegate tasks | Is more comfortable doing tasks personally | Is able to delegate tasks and work as part of a team |
| Spends time with family merely out of obligation; controls family members | Likes to be in charge at family functions | Is able to be intimate with family, yet sees family members as autonomous |
| Experiences a sense of failure if things aren't perfect | Constantly strives for perfection | Takes pleasure when things go well, but it's not a prerequisite for self-esteem |

# Causes

Although genetic or hereditary theories seem to abound for many psychiatric disorders, this is certainly not the case when it comes to controlling perfectionism. Most theorists look at parenting style as being the culprit when it comes to setting the stage for this type of personality disorder. However, we'll also consider anxiety, irrational beliefs, and environment.

## *Parenting Style*

Theodore Millon and Roger Davis (1996) conclude that parental overcontrol is the main reason people develop OCPD. Parental overcontrol differs quite a bit from parental overprotection in that overprotection is usually born of gentle and loving parental concern. Parental overcontrol also differs from parental hostility. Hostile parents punish their children in vitriolic fashion, often without reason or to vent their frustrations or feelings of failure. Overcontrol arises when parents see their role as one of keeping the child in line. The overcontrolling parent is firm and repressive and often holds high standards for the child's behavior in every respect, from grades to table manners. If the child fails to live up to these expectations, punishment is likely to follow. Parental overcontrol is characterized by restrictive child-rearing in which punishment is used to set boundaries, with very little praise or positive reinforcement for good behavior (Millon and Davis 1996).

### Impact in Childhood

Children of overcontrolling parents learn early on to avoid punishment by staying within the boundaries of what's considered acceptable behavior. Because they're punished for wrong behaviors but not praised for right ones, they often learn better what *not* to do. From the perspective of Erik Erikson's (1950) psychosocial theory of development, these children may be more likely to have difficulty with tasks that involve exercising autonomy, initiative, and industry, because they're usually more concerned with behaviors to be avoided. Experience teaches children of overcontrolling parents that in order to please Daddy and Mommy they must do everything right or perfectly—they can't make mistakes, and they must maintain self-control.

> *Frank grew up in a very strict family. His father, a retired Marine colonel, was referred to as "the Great Santini," because just like Robert Duvall as the hard-nosed Marine officer "Bull" Meecham in the movie* The Great Santini, *he treated his wife and children in much the same way that he'd treat new recruits. No one in Frank's family ever stepped out of line or did anything that was considered disrespectful to either parent. When Frank was a senior in high school, his father grounded him for two months and wouldn't let him attend his own prom because he got a "B" in gym class.*

## Impact in Adulthood

As these children mature, what they take from their childhood experience is that it's important to follow the rules, to obey authority, and to keep their behavior in check, otherwise they end up feeling shame, guilt, and tremendous self-doubt.

Thus when these children grow up, they feel a need to keep their behavior under control at all costs. And just as their parents were controlling of them, now they feel they must be controlling of others as well. (This is sometimes referred to as "identifying with the aggressor.") So, they become exactly like their overcontrolling parents. Indeed, most critical adults we've worked with in our private practices have a critical parent with whom they've identified, whether consciously or subconsciously.

> *Alicia grew up in a very strict household where she and her brother were taught to be neat, organized, and clean. They weren't allowed to go out after school to play but instead had to help clean the house and help prepare dinner before their parents came home from work. On Saturdays, when other kids were out playing or*

*going to Little League games, Alicia and her brother would have to help do the laundry and vacuuming. Alicia took many of these traits of fastidiousness and cleanliness into her adolescent and adult years.*

Remember Brad and Ava from the beginning of the chapter? Brad's parents—a dentist and a school principal—had been loving but very strict and orderly in his upbringing. And although Ava's parents are proud of her, they don't express it. Instead they expect the same level of achievement from Ava that they did when she was in high school and college: If she got a "B" it was considered a failure on her part and they told her to work harder. She didn't have much of a social life in high school or college outside of her membership in honor societies and her involvement in student government. She prided herself on being a geek, though, and figured it would all pay off once she got into a top MBA program.

## Anxiety

Another way to think about controlling perfectionism is as a way to alleviate deep-seated anxiety. People who feel inferior or are filled with self-doubt about their credibility or adequacy, such as controlling perfectionists, may respond to these insecurities by trying to control others, thereby allaying or modulating these anxious feelings.

## Irrational Beliefs

Albert Ellis, the founder of a school of psychotherapy called rational emotive therapy, had an interesting theory of how people become controlling perfectionists. Ellis (1979) hypothesized that much of people's psychological or emotional distress is caused by their adherence to certain irrational beliefs. An example of an irrational belief that controlling perfectionists commonly subscribe to is the idea that "one should be thoroughly competent, adequate and achieving in all possible respects if one is to consider oneself worthwhile" (Ellis 1979, p. 63). Ellis concluded that to pursue this illusory goal of perfection resulted in a self-definition that was entirely dependent on external or extrinsic achievements rather than intrinsic value or self-worth. He cautioned that perfectionism leads to fear of taking risks and making mistakes, which often sabotages the very achievement that the perfectionist strives for. Ellis felt that the antidote to this type of irrational thinking is to "do" rather than to always have to "do well," or, if you're trying to "do well," that you do so for your own sake and not to please others or to compete with them.

Another example of an irrational belief (Ellis and Harper 1984) that we feel influences the controlling perfectionist is "It's awful when people don't behave or do as we want them to." This irrational belief speaks to the need to control others. The more rational approach is to accept that people have free will and therefore will do what they want; therefore, it's irrational to expect or demand that others do what you want them to, just because you say so. Finally, Ellis (1979) describes another irrational belief that we feel very much underlies the controlling perfectionist: "the idea that certain people are bad, wicked or villainous and that they should be severely blamed and punished for their villainy" (65). This belief naturally speaks to the moralistic, highly dogmatic controlling perfectionist, the "puritanical compulsive" described earlier.

## Environment

Finally, it's possible that controlling perfectionism may arise as a result of situational or environmental factors other than parenting. This explanation presents itself most often in cases of professionally bound controlling perfectionists. There are certain occupations in which order, control, perfection, and rigid adherence to rules, policies, and procedures are the gold standard for professional behavior. For example, police work involves making certain that the general public adheres to laws and that order and control are maintained. Similarly, a classroom teacher must be able to maintain control over a room full of students. Yet we often see that people in the aforementioned professions have difficulty separating out their professional and personal lives, to the point where they begin to impose the same sort of strict, rigid standards in their personal relationships as in their work. Such is the case with the cop who treats everyone like a suspected criminal or the teacher who treats everyone like a third-grader. We've also seen this phenomenon occur with clergy, military personnel, and people who work in various highly technical occupations that demand adherence to a strict set of rules or policies, like engineering and physical sciences. We discuss this in more detail in subsequent chapters that look at controlling perfectionists in the workplace.

Understanding what causes controlling perfectionists to behave the way they do may be small consolation if you have to deal with one on a daily basis. However, knowing something about the cause of the behavior will come in handy when we discuss strategies for dealing with the controlling perfectionist in your life.

In this chapter we outlined some general characteristics of controlling perfectionists. In the next chapter, we present a detailed picture of what the controlling perfectionist may look like in three different areas of daily life. Thus whether this person is your romantic partner, your parent, or someone in your workplace, you'll learn to recognize the many specific behaviors that relate to the problem of a hypercritical nature.

# CHAPTER 2

........................................

# The Controlling Perfectionist as Romantic Partner, as Parent, and in the Workplace

Our society values and rewards people who are well organized, who are willing to work hard, and who devote
themselves to moral excellence. Therefore, you're bound
to encounter perfectionists in many walks of life. Your doctor,
mechanic, dentist, teacher, or financial advisor may be a perfectionist. Perfectionism can lead to success in many careers. But this
perfectionism can be toxic to other people, especially those who
must interact with a controlling perfectionist day in and day out.
The constant friction created in these types of relationships can
wear down even the most courageous and well-adjusted person;
Albert Bernstein (2001) includes such overbearing and demanding
people in his discussion of "emotional vampires" who drain and
exhaust others.

This chapter deals with controlling perfectionists in the three
settings in which they can do the greatest harm. You can choose to
read only about the setting that most pertains to you currently, but
we recommend you read the entire chapter to get a more complete
picture of the perfectionist in your life. We may describe traits in
one area that also play a role in other areas.

# As Romantic Partner

In the beginning of their courtship, most people would consider a perfectionistic partner a very good catch indeed.

## *Explaining the Perfectionist's Attractiveness*

Here are some reasons you may be attracted to the perfectionist (we'll alternate between male and female pronouns, but most of these apply to either): He's neatly if not meticulously dressed. Her outfits are perfectly coordinated and accessorized. It's clear that he puts a lot of time and money into making himself look good. Her makeup and nails are flawless. He's very well mannered. She's polite. He seems respectful of others. She's articulate and well spoken. He appears to be in control of himself and his emotions all the time. (This is a particularly attractive quality to people who have been in abusive or volatile relationships.) She's responsible. He doesn't smoke. She doesn't drink or do drugs. He's tidy. She's confident. He's reliable. She's self-sufficient. He seems reasonably successful. She's conscientious. He has a good work ethic. She has a good job. He's a saver, not a spender.

### Appearance

Perfectionists take great pride in their personal appearance. They may work out on a regular basis, rising at the break of dawn to run or go to the gym so that they never put on weight. They may have standing appointments for things like manicures and haircuts. If they're going for the executive look, their clothes are carefully starched and pressed; if they're going for a more laid-back look, their clothing has the perfect amount of simulated wear, their shoes just the right amount of scuff. Perfectionists are nothing if not fastidious in their grooming, dress, and personal hygiene. They tend to be very conventional, however. Rarely will perfectionists take a chance on something that goes against fashion or tradition; instead they stick with the tried and true.

## Moral Behavior

Perfectionists always seem to have their act together as far as behaving in ways that are proper, dutiful, and admirable. For example, he regularly visits his great-aunt in the nursing home; she takes her little sister to choir practice every Friday night and goes to church every Sunday. They're always talking about doing "the right thing" and constantly putting down people who do the wrong things (for example: "Can you believe Harrison? The guy never waxes his new car. What's the point of even having one?"). To someone who's looking to marry, a perfectionist would never be unfaithful—heaven forbid! He'd be an attentive husband or she'd be a doting wife. And, what a wonderful father or mother the perfectionist would make: teaching the children important moral values, making sure they're brought up the right way; ensuring they get a proper education; working hard to support the family, formulating budgets and goals.

## Dependability

Importantly, the perfectionist is perceived as highly capable. If you're somewhat directionless in life and have some issues, this is a person who will certainly take over and guide you and get you on the straight and narrow path. In fact, all perfectionists tend to bring out often hidden dependency needs in the people they attract. A person with strong dependency needs might think along the following lines:

- *Here's someone I can lean on for support.*

- *He's a conscientious and hard worker who will manage our money very well.*

- *She's competent and confident and will lead me through life's uncertainties.*

- *He's an excellent judge who will take the weight of making decisions off my shoulders.*

Controlling perfectionists tend to bring out many qualities in people that these people may be unaware of. We address these issues more fully in later chapters.

## Missing Pieces

For a couple of reasons, people who come from dysfunctional or abusive homes might become attracted to controlling individuals, and vice versa. If you grew up in a damaging home environment, healthy self-love is something that you probably never saw displayed, so you never learned it. Therefore, when confronted with a controlling perfectionist who appears to have things under control or who appears to be very disciplined, the tendency is to see that person as having traits that you may feel you are lacking—what you need to make you feel like a whole person worthy of love. This was described brilliantly by Harville Hendrix in the book *Getting the Love You Want* (1988). Hendrix proposes that people generally tend to look to romantic partners to make up for their missing pieces, those parts of themselves that were lost or damaged during childhood. We have also seen this dynamic at play in other types of relationships people choose, such as work relationships or friendships. Hendrix asserts that it's no accident that people are attracted to certain other types of people. If you're lacking in self-discipline, work ethic, goal orientation, or organization and reliability, you might find yourself in the clutches of a controlling perfectionist, having been attracted to these exact same qualities.

Conversely, controlling perfectionists are often quite skilled at picking people whom they can dominate or control. We've also seen instances in which controlling perfectionists are attracted to people who have close, intimate relationships with friends or family and are able to have fun with others. Controlling perfectionists may admire the ability to be intimate and to have fun in relationships and hope to achieve these same things, then become resentful when they find themselves unable.

# Coldness toward You

As the romantic relationship progresses, the perfectionist's reserved nature, which was once attractive, becomes disquieting and problematic. The self-control or self-restraint the perfectionist showed early on now seems to be actually some sort of emotional detachment. Like a Vulcan from *Star Trek*, the perfectionist may be ruled by logic and not seem to understand others' emotional needs. Here are some common complaints:

- "He rarely spontaneously expresses affection."

- "Before having sex, she'll make sure that she's squeaky clean, has applied just the right amount of perfume, and has arranged the bed sheets to perfection; yet her lovemaking seems mechanical, unimaginative, and lacking in passion. She rarely shows signs of arousal."

- "He refuses to say 'I love you,' often defending himself with such verbiage as 'I wouldn't be here if I didn't love you. You know I love you—why do I have to say it?'"

- "She seems distant."

- "He seems to brood a good deal of the time, and although he can be clever and even humorous at times, he never seems genuinely happy."

- "She gets stuck in the same routines and doesn't seem to have time for romance or lovemaking."

- "Our conversations are mundane and 'same-old same-old.'"

# Criticism

If your partner is a perfectionist, as the relationship continues to develop, the two of you may seem to disagree about almost everything. Even when it comes to simple chores like washing dishes or vacuuming, the perfectionist always knows and can demonstrate which way is best and explain why the way *you* do it is poor in comparison. Complicating the matter is the fact that because they have always striven for perfection, perfectionists *are* masters of efficiency and effectiveness at many tasks. Obviously, anyone who spends a good deal of time and effort getting things perfect will, in fact, do things better than someone who nevertheless gets the job done.

But what's good for one person doesn't always work for others. While a perfectionist may, for example, want to clean the house first thing in the morning, someone who's less of a morning person might want to wait until the evening. Furthermore, priorities are notoriously personal. For example, a husband might feel that spending time with the children is more important than cleaning the kitchen, but his perfectionistic and controlling wife may insist that what the children really need is a parent who models correct behavior and that he's setting a poor example by playing a "frivolous" game with them.

Over time, the perfectionist's insistence that things be done "just so" worsens. The perfectionist becomes openly critical, nitpicky, and fussy. If your partner is a perfectionist, you may be subjected to the following types of comments:

- "Do you have to cut your meat into such little pieces?"

- "Why don't you put the magazines back in the rack right after you read them?"

- "Must you brake so hard? You're wearing them out!"

- "Must you chew your food so loudly?"

- "You spent money on *what*? Again?"

In these situations, efforts to defend yourself are useless. For the perfectionist, for everything there's a right way and a wrong way: issue closed, no room for debate or discussion. "You shouldn't brake like that." "Normal people don't cut their meat into tiny, tiny pieces! That's just weird."

The person who once seemed wonderfully sensible and responsible reveals a dark side to these traits: he or she is stingy, prudish, and pedantic. "Why'd you buy such an expensive pair of sneakers? What's the matter with the $20 pair?" "Do we really need to spend $15 on a bottle of wine to bring to the party? Didn't you just meet these people?" The perfectionist may criticize your makeup, your clothing, or your pronunciation or grammar. Your car may be too messy; your phone conversations may be too long. You may be criticized for spending too much time with your friends or family, for watching the wrong sort of movies, or for reading the wrong sort of books. Soon, nothing you do seems good enough. And anything done for the sheer joy of leisure or recreation is seen as just a waste of time. "Why don't you do something productive?" the perfectionist may ask. "Why don't you get up earlier?" "Why don't you go back to school?" "Why don't you take a second job?" It may seem next to impossible for the perfectionist to give up this rigorous attitude and just enjoy life for a little while. Even your vacations with the perfectionist have to be well planned to make the best use of time. And if things don't go as planned due to weather or disagreement, in the perfectionist's mind the vacation is ruined.

In fights and arguments, the perfectionist will often criticize your reactions as "way too emotional" or devoid of any type of logic or common sense. You constantly seem to be defending yourself, but the more you do, the more entangled you become. Worse yet, and infuriatingly, the perfectionist drowns you in corrections that can derail you from addressing the main problem. You say you get out of work at five o'clock, and the perfectionist corrects you by saying actually you get out at ten minutes to five. You say you haven't made love in two weeks, and the perfectionist corrects you by saying technically it's been thirteen days. You claim you left a note on the bulletin board in the late morning, and the perfectionist says no, it was in the early afternoon. And the incessant arguing drives you farther and farther away from each other; all the while your partner denies having done anything wrong and insists that you're the one who has to change.

## *Fear of Intimacy*

A growing number of clinicians and researchers (e.g., Millon and Davis 1996) believe that perfectionism and criticism are actually psychological defense mechanisms for keeping people at a distance. If you think about it, it's very difficult to get close to somebody who's always criticizing you.

Could it be that the controlling perfectionist in your life is actually trying to drive you away, to create a relationship that isn't "too close"? Believe it or not, a fear of intimacy isn't rare among the general population, and it seems to be ubiquitous among perfectionists. Sure, they enjoy sex at times, and they may enjoy spending time with their partners and children, as long as it involves something that they like, things are not too intimate, and things are done their way.

Intimacy requires that you lose yourself to some degree in order to join with another person. For perfectionists, the conditions necessary for intimacy may feel like an unacceptable loss of control or a frightening loss of their own identity. This is another reason many perfectionists are workaholics: it keeps them out of intimate contact with others. Unless these fears are dealt with in some way, a perfectionist stands little chance of ever getting truly close to anyone. We discuss some strategies to manage this fear later in the book (chapter 7).

# As Parent

Of all the kinds of relationships in which one person feels never good enough, none is so insidious as the parent-child dyad. Young children are in so many ways dependent upon their parents, and their day-to-day exposure to their parents' dysfunctions runs a high risk of being life transforming.

## *Outward Focus*

Here's a portrait of a household run by perfectionistic and controlling parents: The parents are community organizers who volunteer to coach and lead Girl Scouts; they almost never miss a parent-teacher conference. These parents teach their children discipline, orderliness, and good moral values. The whole family is well-groomed; the children are famously polite and well-behaved, as well as good students. The lawn is neatly mowed; the house is freshly painted. Everything is in its place. The family car perfectly fits the family configuration.

"What's wrong with that?" you may ask. But a closer look reveals a dysfunctional family pattern. Everything is designed to create an appearance of perfection. The parents may be hell-bent on making their children fit into ideal molds. The parents may hold the children to high standards but give them only criticisms and corrections, not warm encouragement. There may be emphasis on accomplishments, setting goals, and completing chores, but no recognition of a fragile and emerging inner emotional life or a need for age-appropriate social interactions.

Furthermore, such parents' need for control and their insistence on having others do things their way undoubtedly impair their children's quest—so important during adolescence—to establish their own identity. While these parents' desire to keep their children safe and to see them succeed may be admirable, the boundaries and limitations these parents set for their children are uncompromising and inflexible and usually don't account for their children's wishes, talents, or values. Such parents as these may minimize or disapprove of any of a child's gifts and strengths that aren't in line with their goals and vision for the child. Their children are often torn between what they *want* to do and what they *should* do (in an effort to please their parents). Of all the things perfectionistic and controlling parents may do, this is perhaps the worst: not letting their children choose their own direction in life. (Of course, we're talking here about older children and not three-year-olds!)

## Missing the Good

If there's one thing perfectionistic and controlling parents are good at, it's negative evaluation. They often focus on small imperfections in both themselves and others while ignoring the good parts. If something is 99 percent good, they may agonize over the other 1 percent.

This habit of dwelling on the bad while ignoring the good actually seems to be rooted in the deeper, more automatic areas of the perfectionist's *perceptual processes*—the way the brain organizes incoming information from the senses. We've found, for example, that a perfectionist's attention is involuntarily drawn to focus on things that are wrong, no matter how small. Walking into a room, a perfectionist will almost immediately notice the wrinkle in the throw rug or the one piece of wallpaper that's somewhat crooked. When meeting someone new, a perfectionist will immediately catalog imperfections in that person's appearance: a crooked tooth, an unbuttoned button, or perhaps a missed day of shaving.

Sadly, perfectionistic and controlling parents miss out on the enjoyment of the vast majority of good things about their children.

## Conditional Love

Children of critical parents tend to be critical themselves and may grow up to be perfectionistic and controlling parents also. Yet something we also commonly see with children of critical parents is that, recognizing that they can be very critical themselves and disliking their own parents' criticisms, all they do is tell their children how wonderful they are. "Nice job, Joey—way to throw that pass." "I love your new dress, Allison. Did you pick it out yourself? You're just a *phenomenal* dresser." While these kinds of comments are okay once in a while, the problem with this approach when taken too often is that it sends a message to the children that their actions are always being evaluated. Joey and Allison may feel as if parental approval is contingent on their doing well in their parents' eyes—in other words, that their parents' love is conditional. Rather than feel loved simply for who they are, they may grow up feeling as if everything they do is being evaluated, as if they're always under a microscope—and that if they can be evaluated positively, they can also be evaluated negatively. For instance, if Joey throws a pass and his mother says nothing, he may take that as a negative evaluation.

# In the Workplace

As destructive as perfectionistic behavior can be, there's a good deal of reverence for perfectionism in our workaday world. People who are highly organized, neat, respectful, detail oriented, conscientious, and timely are highly valued and often rise to leadership positions. They may be seen as model employees.

## Overfocus on Details

For all of perfectionists' positive traits, they have many pernicious qualities that often make problems for both them and others. Probably the worst is their ability to get lost in details. They may make long and detailed lists and spend countless hours in organization. Often, this trait can make them lose sight of their main goal. One perfectionistic printer, for example, agonized for hours over what typeface he wanted to use in a brochure, leading him to miss the deadline he had agreed to with his client. One perfectionistic salesman would go into the office half an hour early every day to straighten up and make numerous to-do lists for the day. He'd always try to accomplish much more than time allowed, but he'd insist on following every step of his lists. Although his reports were always neatly written and delivered in a timely manner, he wouldn't get around to making sales calls until the late afternoon and was hence the worst salesman in his division.

Needless to say, it can be absolutely agonizing to have to sit through a speech or a set of instructions from a perfectionist. When perfectionists give you driving directions, for example, they may go down endless rabbit trails. Not only is it torture to have to listen to these types of instructions, it's next to impossible to glean the main points of the speech. In a corporate setting, this creates a good deal of confusion and inefficiency. One perfectionistic salesman's internal e-mails were never read, because they were too lengthy. "We see an e-mail from Jim, and we just hit delete," one coworker quipped.

Perfectionists are unusually adept at focusing on what's wrong while ignoring all that's right, a process they engage in with both themselves and others. While correcting employees' oversights and errors may have its place as a management strategy, it makes many perfectionistic and controlling managers "one-trick ponies." Such managers may neglect the use of many other managerial strategies that can be more effectual, such as encouragement, rewards, team-building, and effective use of employees' strengths. Constantly pointing out employees' mistakes may make them angry and resentful and appears to breed a corporate culture of negativity.

## Conformity and Resistance to Change

Newly hired perfectionists are very quick to adapt to the corporate or workplace culture, adopting the dress and jargon. Perfectionists tend to be conformists; in many ways they don't like "rocking the boat." Once they've learned the ropes and polished their performance, they like to stick to their routines. Generally they're not very innovative. In fact, most are likely to resist change even when it would be productive. Change is threatening if it requires perfectionists to do new tasks at which they may not perform to their own consistently high standards.

Sometimes, perfectionists will resist such changes subtly, perhaps passive-aggressively. They may try to sabotage the new implementations by calling in sick on days for which key meetings are scheduled or procrastinating when required to turn in their share of the new project.

## Issues with Time Management

Procrastination may be a form of passive-aggressive resistance, but it's also often the result of a desire to get things perfect. As you might imagine, when you pay attention to each and every detail and insist on excellence in all areas, any project can present an incredible demand on your energies and resources. Thus, a big or new undertaking may paralyze a perfectionist with fear. The perfectionist may worry over details, unable to move forward effectively in this task, until the last possible moments.

This procrastination seems to contradict another characteristic of many perfectionists: an obsession with punctuality. An expectation of timeliness and adherence to schedules is reasonable, but a perfectionist will use others' tardiness or disregard for time as a basis for causing them grief.

> The English faculty at a university had to share a meeting room with the math faculty. The math faculty had the room from 2:00 to 3:00, while the English faculty had it from 3:00 to 4:00. If the math faculty's meeting wasn't finished by 3:00, the English faculty coordinator would storm in anyway, insisting that his fellow English faculty members take seats. In spite of the math faculty coordinator's protests, the English faculty coordinator would simply start his meeting. This eventually led to both faculty coordinators being disciplined.

It may be small surprise to you that the English faculty coordinator was someone who insisted that his professors be in the classroom five minutes early and not teach one minute past the allotted time. Faculty members who adhered to this policy were the ones he recommended for promotion, regardless of their teaching skills.

## *Inflexibility and Overwork*

Yet another problem that we see in organizational settings is perfectionists' insistence that things be done their way. This stubbornness can create a myriad of problems, not least of which is not allowing others to contribute helpful ideas. And if perfectionists aren't willing to let someone do a job possibly less well than they themselves could, they'll end up doing pretty much everything on their own. One perfectionistic and controlling union leader insisted on taking over the ordering of food for meetings, believing she could order much better fare than the secretary whose job it was. To everyone else, the secretary had done a more than adequate job with the food—no one had complained—and ordering food only increased the union leader's level of stress. But she just couldn't stand to see someone do what she perceived to be a lousy job. When one of her friends suggested that she just let the secretary do it, she replied: "If we're lax in one area, we'll be lax in all areas. I don't do second best."

## *The Toll on the Perfectionist*

The constant need for perfection, the tendency to obsess over details, and the desire to do everything because others can't do as good a job as they can create a good deal of stress in perfectionists' lives. Consequently, they're prone to stress-related disorders: headaches, gastrointestinal problems, and muscular problems, such as chronic backaches and jaw problems commonly known as TMJ. Many of these afflictions force perfectionists to miss days of work, which only serves to exacerbate their stress. And while many corporations offer their employees stress-reduction programs or mental health benefits, there are none to our knowledge that actually address the underlying problem of perfectionism.

Although controlling perfectionists can be found in all walks of life, the ones who present the greatest challenges are the ones we love and the ones we work with. Despite their good qualities and even their best intentions, they pose many obstacles to healthy functioning in these types of relationships. Before you can formulate strategies for dealing with the perfectionist in your life, though, you'll need to consider all the ways in which the central message that you're not good enough has affected you. In the next chapter we help you explore the extent of the damage.

# CHAPTER 3

..................

# How the Controlling Perfectionist Has Affected You

In this chapter we help you examine your reactions to the controlling perfectionist in your life. How do you respond internally—emotionally and mentally—to the criticism, and how do you behave as a result? Being able to accurately identify your difficulties with the controlling perfectionist by examining how this person affects you is the beginning of being able to discover real solutions and ways that you can more effectively manage your relationship.

To begin, do any of the following statements seem familiar?

- "Jill is such a pain in the neck to work with on a project. It's like she's always competing with me and everyone on the team. She acts like a know-it-all."

- "It's like Steve is always looking over my shoulder, waiting for me to make a mistake so he can criticize me or put me down."

- "Sandra is so picky. She won't get off my back if I'm even a few minutes late for a lunch date. It's like she can't let go of it...like I've committed some major crime!"

- "When I'm with Henry, like say we're out at a party, I feel like he's my keeper—always on guard about who I'm talking to or what I'm doing. I can't relax and have a good time."

- "At the swim club we belong to, everyone calls Louis 'the Pool Nazi.' He won't let any guests on the premises for even a second if not accompanied by a member, and if one of the kids is a minute late for swim team practice, he makes sure they don't compete in the next meet. Who put *him* in charge of everything?"

- "Trisha is so into neatness and order that no sooner have the kids taken a toy out to play with, she's putting it away and straightening up. She won't give the kids or me a break."

These are just a few examples of the types of statements made by people who deal with a controlling perfectionist on a daily basis. The following stories describe how the influence of a controlling perfectionist can have drastic consequences on the entire future of a family.

*Joan was proud of her reputation as the toughest district attorney in the state. She had made a name for herself as someone who wouldn't plea-bargain a case just to avoid the expense of a trial— she made sure the "bad guys" got what they deserved. However, she also had a reputation among her colleagues as a rigid, moralistic shrew who loved to do things that got her name in the newspapers no matter whom it hurt.*

*In one of her well-known cases Joan had prosecuted Tara, a single mother of two young children whose boyfriend was a cocaine user. When the boyfriend was busted for dealing, Joan also went after Tara. She wanted to make an example of Tara and try to obtain the maximum sentence for cocaine possession and distribution. This meant that Tara, who had no prior record, was facing a minimum of ten to fifteen years in prison. Because Tara had no relatives willing to look after her children, they were taken into the custody of child protective services. Tara was denied pre-trial intervention and also was denied the option of going into a drug treatment program in which she could be eventually reunited with her children, who ended up in foster homes.*

*When Tara was sentenced, it made all the newspapers. Joan commented in an interview that she believed that the best interests of society had been served in this case and that the children of her state should not be exposed to drug-abusing parents. Yet attorneys familiar with the case thought that Joan was grandstanding in order to gain publicity and that the punishment definitely did not fit the crime.*

Joan is the epitome of a professionally bound controlling perfectionist. Her career and her self-identity are essentially one and the same. She prides herself on her high standards when it comes to morality and ethics, which was evident in her approach to Tara's case. The fact that Joan refused to be dissuaded by the human aspects of the case reveals her rigidity and her hard-heartedness— her seeming inability to show any pity or kindness. Joan also lacks insight into her own behavior—a common shortcoming of controlling perfectionists—as evidenced in her inability to see how she was grandstanding, which was clear to her colleagues. Tara paid a high price indeed for Joan's inflexibility and righteousness.

*When she and Tom became engaged, Julie was thrilled and couldn't wait to tell her friends and family. She had been dating Tom for three years, and although they had talked about marriage, it had always seemed like just a dream. Julie's parents were thrilled that Tom and Julie had decided to tie the knot. Julie's mother was especially excited, and she looked forward to planning the wedding with Julie.*

*Julie and her mother discussed an outdoor wedding with an informal reception. Plans were going great until Tom's mother, Hilda, got into the act. Hilda didn't want to hear anything about a wedding that wouldn't be held in a church. She also felt strongly that only a formal reception was in keeping with her standards. When her efforts at control didn't seem to work, Hilda was infuriated, and she directed her anger at Julie, who began to feel so frustrated that she and Tom considered simply eloping. At one point, Hilda pretty much said that unless she had a say in the wedding plans, she wouldn't attend the ceremony. Tom's parents were divorced, and, given how contentious their divorce had been, Tom's father didn't want to try to be a voice of reason or negotiate a compromise with his ex-wife. What he'd learned over the years was that you'd save yourself a lot of grief if you just gave Hilda her way.*

*Exasperated by Hilda's stubborn behavior, Tom and Julie decided to get married by the mayor in a small civil ceremony and then went out with a few friends and even fewer family members afterward. Julie and Hilda didn't speak to one another for years.*

We've all heard of debacles like this, and it's hard not to feel bad for couples like Tom and Julie who were initially so happy to share their wedding day with their friends and family. Hilda's rigidity and her sense of the moral thing to do (have a proper church wedding) far surpassed the notion that this was supposed to be Tom and Julie's day, not hers. Hilda's my-way-or-the-highway approach showed her lack of compassion for her son and future daughter-in-law. Hilda also had in her mind a perfect wedding and was unwilling to consider anything that didn't conform to this perspective. It might not surprise you to learn that Hilda's constant efforts to browbeat others into submission had contributed to the demise of her marriage to Tom's father.

## Elizabeth Packard

On May 21, 1839, Elizabeth Parsons Ware married the Reverend Theophilus Packard Jr., a strict Calvinist minister, in Massachusetts. Although they had six children and moved around, finally settling in Illinois, for many years their life together was fairly quiet—until Elizabeth began to express opinions that differed from her husband's on matters of religion and slavery. Theophilus couldn't tolerate her dissenting views. Under Illinois state law, it was possible for a husband to have his wife committed to a mental hospital against her will without a public hearing. So with the help of a Dr. J. W. Brown, who posed as a sewing-machine salesman in order to conduct his surreptitious evaluation of Elizabeth's mental stability, on June 18, 1860, the minister had his wife taken into custody and confined in a state mental hospital for the next three years. Once she was finally able to petition for a jury trial, it took the jury only seven minutes to decide that she had been unjustly confined and should be freed immediately.

# Can You See What It's Doing to You?

Several years ago, Al-Anon (the international support group for spouses, partners, and family members of alcoholics) created a TV advertisement that would usually air at around two or three in the morning, a time when the viewer might be waiting for an alcoholic to come home from the bars. The ad began with a couple arguing, presumably after the man had come home intoxicated. The woman is screaming at the man and is totally exasperated. At the end of the ad, the voice-over calmly says: "You can see what drinking is doing to them. Can you see what it's doing to you?" The same question applies to those living with, working with, or otherwise interacting with controlling perfectionists. You can very well see what controlling perfectionism is doing to the people who have to deal with Jill, Steve, Sandra, Henry, Louis, and Trisha (from the beginning of the chapter) and what it did to Tara, Tom, Julie, and Elizabeth Packard, but when *you're* dealing with a controlling perfectionist, whether it be in a love relationship, in a work relationship, or as a friend or family member, the impact tends to be much larger than you're aware of.

Certainly you have some inkling of the effect of the controlling perfectionist on you; otherwise you wouldn't be reading this book. But what so often becomes clear with the clients we counsel is just how pervasive and devastating the influence of the controlling perfectionist is on their feelings and thinking. Our clients often report that they feel as if they've been brainwashed by this person, sometimes over the course of years, and their counseling becomes a way of "deprogramming" them. What they also tell us is that they find themselves acting differently around the controlling perfectionist, almost as if they develop an alter ego. They find that they're not being themselves or allowing their natural personality to come out. Controlling perfectionists are often contentious and seem to thrive on conflict. That's often part of a need to engage in one-upmanship so that they can prove their worth or prove that they're smarter than or superior to others. What friends, family, and coworkers find

**45**

is that it really becomes tedious to interact with a controlling perfectionist because they find themselves always on guard. In other words, controlling perfectionists are just difficult to be around. To get some perspective on this, imagine talking with a friend or coworker whose company you enjoy: you talk about your weekend, talk about a movie you saw recently, and share a joke. The conversation feels light and easy, doesn't it? Now contrast this with your interactions with the controlling perfectionist, in which you may feel as if you're being cross-examined for a crime you didn't commit. You weigh every word; you stutter or stammer. These conversations are anything but light and easy.

# Your Feelings

Although it's important to keep in mind that no one can *make* you feel a certain way, let's explore some of the emotions that the controlling perfectionist may trigger and how this may affect the way you feel about yourself.

## EXERCISE: How Have My Feelings Been Affected?

Check any of the following statements with which you agree concerning the controlling perfectionist in your life.

_____ I often feel inferior.

_____ I often feel demeaned by things this person says about me or by his or her put-downs.

_____ I often feel criticized in front of others.

_____ I always end up feeling like I'm wrong, even when I know I'm right.

_____ I often find myself agreeing or giving in, just to avoid an argument.

_____ I sometimes find myself feeling trapped in the relationship, like I can't be my own person or have my own opinions.

_____ I feel like I'm being micromanaged.

_____ I feel like I don't have much control over my own life whenever I'm in contact with this person.

_____ I constantly feel like I'm being judged.

_____ I feel like I don't have much control over my own social life because this person is critical of my friends or family, so we socialize only with people this person wants to socialize with.

_____ I feel that this person is always lecturing me about something I've done wrong, or how I should act, or what I should and shouldn't say. I feel like a little child being scolded.

_____ I feel dismissed, like I'm not allowed to have my own opinions, and when I do express an opinion I'm criticized for not thinking the same way this person does.

_____ I feel angry or even enraged when this person criticizes me or points out something I've done wrong or a mistake I've made.

Take a look at the items you've checked. If you checked four or more, the controlling perfectionist is likely having a profound impact on how you feel about yourself. Even people who've grown up in loving homes, with loving parents and siblings; even very bright, talented people may find themselves feeling inferior, demeaned, or worthless in the eyes of a controlling perfectionist.

# Your Thinking

How you feel about yourself as a result of interactions with the controlling perfectionist in your life may have an impact on your self-perception and your overall self-esteem. For example, if you find yourself feeling inferior when the controlling perfectionist treats you in a demeaning way or speaks to you in a derogatory tone, over time you may come to think of yourself as inferior. These changes in thinking are often subtle at first; however, they tend to become more pervasive over time. Sadly, you may eventually come to see yourself as the controlling perfectionist does: not smart enough, not talented enough, or not loving enough. This is what our clients mean when they allude to brainwashing. Subjected to harsh judgment and constant criticism, people may be led to believe they have no gifts or talents—nothing to offer.

*Dina was so excited when she was accepted into her first-choice graduate school. She knew how prestigious the graduate program was, and she was even more excited when she was chosen to be a graduate assistant for Dr. Davis. Dr. Davis was someone Dina had admired from the first time she heard her speak at a national conference.*

*Working for Dr. Davis, however, was more than Dina had bargained for. No matter how much work Dina did, no matter how hard she tried, Dr. Davis was extremely critical and demeaning of Dina and the work she did. Dina knew that Dr. Davis was a tough professor with very high standards, but what she didn't know was that Dr. Davis totally lacked compassion.*

*Dina began to think that maybe she wasn't up to the standards of the graduate program and perhaps the admissions office had made a mistake by allowing her into the program and giving her an assistantship with the notable Dr. Davis. Dina's work began to slip and her grades began to drop. By Thanksgiving, Dina was convinced that she was unworthy of being in graduate school. She began to think of herself as a screw-up who was academically unprepared to do graduate-level work.*

Dina's situation is not atypical and exists not only in academic settings, but also in many work situations. If Dr. Davis fits the profile of the controlling perfectionist, Dina could have done Nobel Prize–worthy research and Dr. Davis still would have found fault with it. That's what controlling perfectionists do. There's a difference between a coach or teacher who challenges you to be the best you can be, or someone who encourages you to work to your potential, and someone who holds unrealistically high standards, such as Dr. Davis. It's no wonder that Dina came to doubt herself and her abilities.

## *EXERCISE:* How Has My Thinking Been Affected?

Check any of the following thoughts you often have in your relationship with the controlling perfectionist in your life:

_____ *I must be inferior or stupid.*

_____ *I'm being humiliated on purpose.*

_____ *I can never change the situation.*

_____ *No matter what I do, I can never compete with this person.*

_____ *The relationship never goes my way because of my own defects.*

_____ *No matter what I do, I'll never be able to change the relationship.*

_____ *I'm stupid for staying in the relationship and for not getting out sooner.*

_____ *This person is gifted or talented and I must support him or her.*

_____ *Even though I feel demeaned by this person, I still feel attracted to him or her or want his or her approval.*

_____ *Being around this person will somehow benefit me.*

**49**

Look over the items you've checked. Can you see instances in which the controlling perfectionist has shaped the way you think about yourself? Have you reached certain conclusions about yourself or come to see yourself differently as a result of influence by the controlling perfectionist?

...............................................................................................................

# Your Behavior

Controlling perfectionists have a unique talent for imposing their expectations on others, and what's amazing is that most people will take on these expectations or try to adhere to them even if the standard or expectation seems to go against their nature. Although changes in behavior are subtle at first, most people report that when dealing with a controlling perfectionist, they often make concessions or say and do things that they wouldn't ordinarily.

There are some people who will do anything to keep the peace, whether at work or at home. A "good daughter" will find herself striving to meet her perfectionistic father's expectation that she get into the best college; a "good son" will date only someone his perfectionistic mother approves of. It might seem wise for someone who works for a controlling perfectionist to try to live up to the boss's expectations in order to curry favor or to win promotions or raises. Yet of course these people all end up feeling that whatever they say, whatever they do, it's just not good enough in the eyes of the controlling perfectionist.

> Valerie always managed to be the chair of committees of the parent-teacher organization in her kid's school. It wasn't so much that other parents declined to volunteer for these committees but rather that they got to a point where it was easier to let Valerie chair the committees and do the work.
>
> Last spring, some of the parents wanted to put on a fundraising event to sponsor a special musical program that was touring the area. Many of the parents thought that this would be a good way of exposing the children to classical music without the expense of taking them to a concert hall in a nearby city. Valerie

*hastily rejected the proposal, claiming that no child would want to go to such a concert—her children didn't like classical music.*

*Many parents ended up resigning from Valerie's committee. Others concluded that if things weren't done exactly to Valerie's specifications she'd throw a hissy fit and eventually they'd get to the point where it just wasn't worth fighting for their opinion or views to be heard.*

People like Valerie are particularly hard to deal with. When people volunteer to participate on a committee or to become the chairperson of a committee, they don't expect to be constantly doing battle to get their opinions heard. Yet people like Valerie have a knack for taking charge, and somehow it seems they're always right and everyone else is wrong. A common response in this situation is to sooner or later give in or give up.

## *EXERCISE:* How Has My Behavior Been Affected?

Ask yourself whether you've done the following things in your relationship with the controlling perfectionist in your life. Check all that apply.

_____ Refused to participate in situations in which I might have had contact with this person

_____ Declined invitations to parties or social events to which I knew this person would be invited

_____ Held back on giving my own opinion in order to avoid a conflict

_____ Baited this person into arguments or purposely defended a position I didn't hold, just to get a reaction

_____ Agreed with this person even when my opinion differed, in order to avoid a fight or argument

_____ Gave in to this person's demands rather than saying no, but then ended up kicking myself

_____ Tried to make everything perfect or exactly how this person wanted it, in order to please or gain favor

_____ Sought out the company of others instead of this person so I could be more relaxed or just be myself

..................................................................................................

Controlling perfectionists often affect how people feel about themselves, think, and behave. And, we're sorry to say, controlling perfectionists are probably not going to fundamentally change how they treat others, including you (deep inside, you may have already known that). But here's the good news: you can change how *you* think and behave, and that's precisely what we cover in part II of this book.

# PART II

Practical Strategies

..........................................

# CHAPTER 4

# Recognizing What You Can and Can't Do

To review: For controlling perfectionists, conscientiousness, following the rules, and maintaining high standards are of utmost importance. Because of their tendency to think in terms of right versus wrong, black and white, all or none, controlling perfectionists often feel justified in imposing their will on others, believing that their way of doing things is the one true correct way. It may appear at first glance that controlling perfectionists try to exert control just for the sake of having power over others, and sometimes that's certainly the case. However, there are other times when controlling perfectionists exert control in order to allay their own anxieties: they fear that if others don't adhere to their way of doing things, then chaos will surely follow.

True controlling perfectionists are extremely good at inducing others to submit to their way of doing things by making them feel inferior. Whether through open criticism or more subtle or passive-aggressive expressions of displeasure (a disapproving glance, a certain tone of voice), they constantly call attention to others' perceived faults and failings. Under this kind of scrutiny, most people will try to do better in the controlling perfectionist's eyes. However, those who have to deal with a controlling perfectionist on a day-to-day basis are bound to feel that they're never good enough or that no matter what they do, they can't satisfy or please this person.

They end up exasperated by the negativity, the many demands, and the merciless expectation of perfection in every area.

Given that you're reading this book, you're probably one of these unfortunate people. So, what can you do about it? The first thing you should do is stop trying to change another person, even if that person's behavior is the problem.

# You Can't Change a Controlling Perfectionist

If you're like most people in this situation, in all probability you've made yourself bone-weary in attempts to change the controlling perfectionist in your life. At first you probably asked this person nicely to stop criticizing you. You defended yourself logically, yet the controlling perfectionist kept on. Most likely, you then raised the ante, telling this person that many of his or her behaviors were very disturbing to you and that he or she needed to make significant changes in appreciation and consideration of you. Perhaps this had the desired result—for a while. Maybe at first you were forgiving when the controlling perfectionist returned to his or her ways, but when it happened again and again you began to get angry and—as time went on—even bitter. You tried to shut this person out as best as you could, to ignore the criticism and controlling behavior. But that didn't work either. And now, exhausted, you're coming to the realization that despite your massive efforts, the controlling perfectionist can't be changed. It's unfortunate, but many of us have to reach our endpoint before we realize that trying to change someone is a fruitless endeavor. You can't change another person's nature; you can't convince someone to let go of a general need for perfectionism and control. This person will always be a controlling perfectionist. Period.

# You Can Change Your Interpretations

To reclaim your life, you'll have to change the way the controlling perfectionist affects you. One of the first things you should try to do is expel the idea that to be criticized must always make you feel bad. When someone criticizes you with a remark, you may feel sad, disappointed, embarrassed, frustrated, or angry. You may feel as though you're inferior in some way. But you should be aware of the fact that in spite of the content of the remark, it's really up to you to determine how you'll interpret it. It's your interpretation of the remark, rather than the person making it, or even the remark itself, that affects the way you feel. For example, what if you didn't take it personally? Imagine being criticized and thinking: *I wonder what's wrong with her today? She seems to be in a very negative mood. Perhaps she's having a bad day. Maybe I can cheer her up!* It's plain that this type of interpretation would lead to more positive feelings. You may not be able to control what the controlling perfectionist says and does, but you're clearly in control of your own feelings. One of the things this book will help you do is interpret the controlling perfectionist's actions in a way that's more accurate than you have in the past. More accurate interpretations will lead to more positive feelings (Beck and Freeman 1990)

Contrast the following two stories.

*Fred was a data processor in a payroll company. He was known as a loyal and dutiful employee who was serious about his work.*

*Nevertheless, prior to his semiannual performance evaluation, Fred began to worry about the possibility of his receiving a negative evaluation. He began to lose sleep and not eat. On the day of his evaluation, he literally became ill but forced himself to go into work anyway and receive what he knew would be bad news. Although he received an excellent review overall, his supervisor said that he needed improvement in one area: communicating more effectively with his coworkers. In spite of this one low mark, he received the maximum pay raise allowable.*

*Nevertheless he was devastated and, in the weeks that followed, he allowed the single negative aspect of his evaluation to eat at him, even to the point that he thought about quitting. Although friends tried to reassure him that everyone got at least one low mark, it was no consolation to him.*

*Roy was a union leader in a fragrance manufacturing company. One year during negotiations, his union threatened to go on strike due to the seemingly poor work conditions and lack of pay increases and benefits.*

*The events leading up to the strike were very contentious. The union called a sick-out, costing the company thousands of dollars in lost revenue. At times, relations between labor and management teetered on the edge of violence, with both sides shouting at each other and union representatives blocking the paths of those who wanted to break the picket line.*

*By some miracle, the two sides finally reached an agreement. As they were signing the final contracts, Roy was called into the back room with the company's president and the governing board. Roy was allowed to bring the union vice president in with him. The president and board members berated Roy for his actions during the disaccord. At times, the attacks became personal: he was insulted and sworn at. Roy remained calm, simply nodding his head. By the time the president and board members had exhausted themselves nearly an hour later, silence filled the room. Roy looked up and asked, "Can we go now?" Exasperated by his lack of response to their criticisms, the president and board members simply nodded.*

*As Roy and the union VP walked away from the meeting, Roy was quiet. Bewildered, the VP asked, "How could you have listened to all those foul things they said about you and not get angry?" Roy explained: "I know who I am and I know where I come from. Those people know nothing about me."*

If criticism is by nature hurtful, as Fred's story seems to illustrate, why wasn't Roy hurt?

The answer seems to lie in Roy's *interpretation* of the criticism. He knew that the criticisms were incorrect because he had solid knowledge of himself and his background. In other words, he had a lifelong historical conception of his own personality and motives. He understood that he knew himself better than anyone.

On the other hand, not only did Fred believe that his supervisor must know him better than he knew himself, he took the criticism to mean that he was a bad employee or even that he was defective in some way as a human being, none of which was intended. He read into the criticism more than was there.

One of psychology's greatest contributions is the idea that our beliefs and personal interpretations of events that happen to us affect our feelings and actions. If you believe, for example, that the woman who cut you off while you were driving intended to hurt you in some way, you might become very angry. But if you believe that she was simply in a rush (perhaps she just had to go to the bathroom!), you might find yourself feeling a lot more forgiving. People in identical situations may interpret events very differently.

So you need to ask yourself, *What do I believe about the controlling perfectionist's criticisms of me?* Do you believe that this person is an expert in human behavior or perhaps an expert on your motives? Does this person know more about your intentions than you do? Do this person's criticisms mean that you're defective in some way? If this person criticizes your driving, does that make him or her an expert on driving habits? (If so, why isn't this person a design consultant for an automobile manufacturer?)

Remember, you might not be able to control the controlling perfectionist's need to criticize, but you can control what you believe about it and how you respond to it.

......................................................................................

# *EXERCISE:* Discovering Your Own Negative Interpretations

It will be useful for you to clarify some of your own interpretations. Remember, negative interpretations can lead to negative feelings. More accurate interpretations will lead to more positive feelings.

Put check marks next to the items that best reflect your thinking under the given circumstances involving the controlling perfectionist in your life.

_____ When this person becomes critical, I often believe I'm stupid.

_____ This person's criticisms make me believe that I'm inadequate.

_____ I believe that I'm inferior to this person in many areas.

_____ I think that this person's criticisms are almost always valid.

_____ I believe that this person's approval is critical for me to feel good about myself.

_____ In the past, I've believed that if I made strong efforts I could change this person.

_____ I believe that if I stand up to this person, it will most likely make things worse.

_____ In the past, I've believed that I'm helpless to defend myself when I'm in the presence of this person.

_____ This person's remarks to me often made me believe that I was defective in some way.

_____ When I'm being criticized by this person, I often believe that I have to make changes in myself.

These are all common irrational thoughts and beliefs of people in a relationship with a controlling perfectionist. While we're all prone to making negative and inaccurate interpretations of situations with difficult people, if you checked off four or more statements, this suggests that you may indeed have a tendency to make negative interpretations and often blame yourself for the nature of the controlling perfectionist. Checking off even one means that there are areas in which you could make changes to improve the way you feel.

......................................................................................

# You Can Change the Nature of Your Relationship

By changing your own behavior and personal interpretations and beliefs about the controlling perfectionist, you can actually change the very quality of your relationship.

For instance, you don't have to go around walking on pins and needles and feeling like you're under a microscope whenever the controlling perfectionist is around. Once you understand that this person's perfectionistic and critical nature are personality flaws and really have nothing to do with you, you'll respond very differently. The recognition that the criticisms really don't have much to do with you gets you out of defensive mode and frees you to respond with more creative and effective measures.

As an interesting aside, you should take note of a truth about constant criticism: logically, it can't all be valid. Think of how the controlling perfectionist is always critical of you. If the criticisms truly had merit, there would be periods of time, such as when you were doing very well by other people's standards, that this person would stop criticizing you. You've most likely noticed that this has never happened!

# You Can Choose Your Battles

Once you change your interpretations and understand that controlling perfectionists' criticisms of you have less to do with you and more to do with their personality, you'll find that you're less emotionally reactive to the criticism. From here, you'll be able to be more thoughtful and make better use of your energy by concentrating on areas in which you feel more productive and rewarded. You'll also notice a dramatic decline in the frequency of negative interactions.

For instance, you might not be able to change—or even influence, for that matter—the fact that your husband constantly complains about how little money you both have, but you certainly might be able to influence the fact that he constantly compares your cooking to his previous wife's. How? Refuse to cook for him.

One good rule of thumb is to choose to fight battles in which you truly have control. Your coworker, for example, might complain that you talk too loudly, make too many phone calls, keep your desk too messy, and have too many people walking in and out to speak with you. These things might make your coworker miserable, but really she's helpless to control or change them. These are things that *you're* in control of. Sure, you might choose to be accommodating and speak more softly. But the point here is that you don't have to. And if you decide to speak loudly, there really isn't much your coworker can do about it. Take some time now to consider the many things that perhaps you haven't realized you control entirely. Other people can complain that you eat too quickly, drive too slowly, and even take too long in the bathroom. But there isn't really much they can do about it, is there?

You don't need to be nasty when you assert your control, just firm and resolved. You may "do battle" in a very polite manner and without sarcasm or condescension. For example, if your coworker tells you that you're talking too loudly, you may reply: "I am so sorry. I know that this is disturbing to you. But this is the way I talk; I don't think I can change it. I think that how loud a person speaks is really a matter of taste and what is loud to one person isn't loud enough to another. We're all different." Your coworker might be angry at your refusal to change, but as you've now indicated, this is her problem, not yours.

Save your energy by ignoring those areas over which you have less control, such as the controlling perfectionist's interactions with third parties (for example, don't ask, "Why did you correct the gas station attendant's grammar?"). This will greatly reduce the number of arguments in your relationship and help you achieve greater gains in other areas. Try to concentrate on those areas that mean the most to you. Let go of the others, even if just until the most important one is resolved. Stay positive. You can be polite, but be persistent. Focus on areas in which you've been successful previously or in areas in which you see the possibility of the controlling perfectionist yielding some control.

Comments like "Must you be so [critical, judgmental, strict, etc.]?" or "Must you be such a [perfectionist, control freak, cheapskate, etc.]?" are bound to be unproductive. Remember, you can't change the controlling perfectionist's personality. Your focus should be on winning individual battles, with specific outcomes, rather than trying to win the whole war at once. For example, concentrate on getting your girlfriend to spend more money on a birthday present rather than trying to convince her to be less stingy in general. Tell your boyfriend that his remarks about your waistline make you feel unsexy and unloving toward him instead of telling him simply to stop being so critical of your appearance. You'll be more successful this way.

Finally, don't give up too soon. Be willing to back off for a while but to come back to the fight later. Prepare yourself for a long battle. Don't "lose it" or become verbally aggressive. Keep working. You'll find yourself much less frustrated if you understand that these things take time. When you choose your battles, every confrontation is like an investment. Eventually it will pay off!

## *EXERCISE:* Choosing Your Battles

Think of some areas of disagreement or some things that you've fought over with the controlling perfectionist in your life. Consider whether, using some of the ideas you've learned in this book, your efforts can be put to productive use in these areas. First, list those issues you can most likely assert control over. Then list those issues over which, at least in the short term, you might only waste your energy.

I feel that I can gain victories in the following areas:

1. _____

_____.

2. _____

_____.

3. _____

_____ .

I feel that these are areas that I should just let go of for now:

1. _____

_____ .

2. _____

_____ .

3. _____

_____ .

..............................................................................................

# You Can Clarify Your Goals

One of the reasons that many people find themselves knuckling under to a controlling perfectionist is that they're not really clear in what their goals are. For many of us, our goals get all jumbled up when we're frustrated by criticism. Ask yourself what usually guides your actions in response to the controlling perfectionist's criticisms. What's driving you? What are you trying to accomplish? Are you defending your honor? Are you trying to correct the controlling perfectionist's misperceptions? Are you trying to appear intelligent? Are you trying to fix the wounded nature of the controlling perfectionist? Having an agenda like one of these can often sabotage your interactions with a controlling perfectionist because it puts too much importance on that person's judgments or keeps you from being an equal director of the interaction.

> Monica was a sales manager who had to submit a quarterly report
> to the regional manager, who was a controlling perfectionist. All
> that Monica really needed was to obtain the regional manager's

*signature on the report. But she also had a desire to be acknowledged and recognized by the authority figures in her life, so after she submitted the report, she called the regional manager to talk about all the time and effort she put into it, hoping to get some kind of kudos or recognition. When the regional manager, always stingy with compliments to anyone, didn't feed her need, Monica became angry and argumentative, forcing the issue to the point where the regional manager refused to approve the report until Monica had made improvements to it.*

By setting well-defined goals, and by concentrating all of your efforts on and directing all your conversation toward these goals, you'll become proactive and not reactive. In other words, you won't feel like a victim anymore. You'll feel empowered and strong. In the example above, the only thing Monica really needed was a signature. But she sabotaged her achievement of this goal with a hidden agenda of wanting express recognition of her work.

Your goals should of course be healthy and achievable ones. They should be specific and not global (for example, *I want her to come to my office picnic*—which is specific—rather than *I want her to participate in my work life*—which is a more global and more difficult goal). They should be clear in your head when you approach the controlling perfectionist. You'll thus find that your interactions are far less entangled and more productive.

Following are some examples of unhealthy goals:

- *I want his approval so that I can feel good about myself.*

- *I want to please her so that I'll look good in the eyes of others.*

- *I want to be in a relationship in which someone is always telling me what to do.*

- *I want to feel that he's wrong and I'm right.*

- *I want her to love me, and I can do it only by appeasing her.*

Here are some healthier goals that are more achievable:

- *I want to get him to turn his work in on time.*

- *I want to work out a parenting plan that works for both of us. I think I can start with asking him to pick up and drop off the children.*

- *I want to get him to show me more affection after sex.*

- *I want to be able to do more fun activities with her. I think I can get her to go for walks on the beach with me.*

- *I want to stop feeling so sad all the time in this relationship after a fight or argument.*

Here's what makes these goals achievable. First, they're healthy for both you and the other person. They don't tear the other person down. They don't try to build up your self-esteem at the other person's cost. They're not belittling to you.

Second, these goals contain reasonable expectations. They're not just pipe dreams or pies in the sky; they're all doable.

Next, they're specific and not global. They focus on an area of the relationship rather than trying to change the *nature* of the relationship itself and all at once. They're limited in their scope and therefore more achievable.

Finally, and most important, they focus on *your* behavior. Trust us—you'll achieve much more when you take it upon yourself to work toward change. You'll find yourself less frustrated and exhausted, more hopeful and empowered.

# You Can Create Space between You and a Controlling Perfectionist

In some cases, it might be possible to put some space between you and the controlling perfectionist in your life. For example, if you don't live with your perfectionistic and controlling parent, you can simply choose to call less often. Or instead of visiting this parent for two days, you can cut it down to one day. We've known people whose parents were so demanding and critical that they actually moved out of state to get some distance and some measure of freedom. While your situation may or may not allow for these types of actions, here are some examples of how people have created space between themselves and a controlling perfectionist, to reduce the frequency of or limit interaction:

- A woman successfully requested that her boss take her out of a workgroup with a controlling perfectionist.

- A high school student changed sports to get away from a particularly critical coach.

- A warehouse manager who constantly bickered with his parts manager whenever he requested parts began to order the parts by mail instead.

- A high school faculty member would simply go the other way when being approached by a particular colleague.

- A woman who found that her tennis partner would criticize her performance on the court when they went to lunch afterward simply made herself more unavailable for these lunches.

- A college student with a perfectionistic and controlling roommate requested a different dorm room.

- A man who dreaded visiting his querulous and overcritical father in the nursing home created distance by making sure that they always shared a meal together during his visit. His father found it hard to talk with his mouth full!

Something simple you can do to create space is refuse to let yourself be drawn into arguments that have no logical solution or outcome. Remember, controlling perfectionists are extremely judgmental, and no matter what the facts are, they feel convinced that their opinions are right and anyone who disagrees is therefore wrong. Avoid conversations involving religion, politics, or other areas in which the controlling perfectionist has strong views.

Creating space whenever possible is an easy way to limit the impact that the controlling perfectionist has on your life. As such, it's just one way to set effective boundaries and limit the damage that the controlling perfectionist can do.

So, although it may be impossible to change someone, you can change the nature of your relationship with that person. You can change the way you think and react, you can choose your battles, and you can define your own agendas. You can stop being a victim of the controlling perfectionist.

The point is that even though you can't directly change the controlling perfectionist's behavior, you can change how it affects you and also act in ways that are likely to create different and better outcomes. Your new ways of responding may even have a desirable effect on the controlling perfectionist's behavior. There's an old expression: "You can lead a horse to water, but you can't make him drink." But as one wag once added, "Yes, but you can make the horse very thirsty!" In the same way, your "undercover ops" for dealing with the controlling perfectionist can help you win battles. In the next chapter, we discuss means of setting limitations and boundaries in your relationship with the controlling perfectionist that you can use in any situation and whenever creating space might not be possible or practical. In chapter 6, we teach you strategies for better communication to help you achieve your healthy and specific objectives.

# CHAPTER 5

......................................

# Setting Limits and Boundaries

The controlling perfectionist in your life may be micromanaging you or bullying you into doing things that you really don't want to or that you feel obligated to do. When you're in daily contact with a controlling perfectionist, it's important that you limit this kind of behavior; otherwise you risk this person running your life and denying you any kind of consideration, not to mention impoverishing your sense of who you are. This means that at times you need to come to your own defense or challenge unreasonable expectations. However, you need to be careful to do so in ways that won't create more problems for you than they solve. Responding too aggressively or making the controlling perfectionist angry might have negative consequences—you don't want to do something you'll regret. For example, it may be unwise to storm into your boss's office and tell her to shove her job, unless you can afford to be unemployed. You can avoid such desperate situations in the first place if you define and make clear to the controlling perfectionist what you will and won't put up with.

By setting limits or boundaries on inappropriate or abusive behavior, you're essentially saying, "It's not okay to treat me this way." This becomes a way of asserting yourself and claiming your self-worth because you're also communicating that you deserve to be treated better. Limits and boundaries are necessary to any healthy relationship, but with a controlling perfectionist you may need to work harder to enforce them.

In this chapter, we suggest some ways you can begin to set limits and boundaries on perfectionistic and controlling behaviors so that you may have more freedom and hopefully more happiness in any kind of relationship with a controlling perfectionist. (In chapters 7 and 8 we present additional strategies specific to handling controlling perfectionists in romantic relationships, in family relationships, and in the workplace.)

# Difficulties with Boundary Setting

It's not uncommon for people who have a history of being treated poorly or abusively to have difficulty accepting that they deserve to be treated better. The following exercise will help you determine whether the controlling perfectionist may find your boundaries weak or lacking as a result of damage to your self-worth.

## *EXERCISE:* Discovering Origins of Difficulties with Boundary Setting

So that you may explore the possible roots of your problems with the controlling perfectionist, answer the following questions as they relate to your childhood and adolescence. In the space provided for each, write the number that best corresponds to your answer, where 0 = never, 1 = sometimes, and 2 = often.

Did you feel that either of your parents invalidated your thoughts or feelings?  _____

Did either of your parents yell at, scream at, criticize, or verbally abuse you?  _____

Was either of your parents physically abusive of you?  _____

Do you feel that your parents neglected your emotional needs or didn't provide much love or nurturing? _____

Did your parents neglect to take you for regular medical and dental checkups? _____

Were you physically or sexually abused by anyone? _____

Did you feel rejected or unloved by one or both of your parents? _____

Were you ridiculed, belittled, or made fun of? _____

Did your parents threaten to send you away, for instance to live with a relative or to a boarding school? _____

Did you witness physical or sexual abuse of a family member? _____

Now add up your score. A score of 0 indicates you probably grew up in a healthy environment in which your needs were addressed and you developed good self-worth. A score between 10 and 20 indicates you probably grew up in a home that was abusive or neglectful or, at the very least, invalidating. People who score high on this measure usually have difficulty setting boundaries and limits with controlling perfectionists because they have difficulty valuing and loving themselves.

# Valuing Yourself and Increasing Your Self-Worth

If you suffer from a lack of self-worth, the good news is that there are things you can do to help you value yourself and recognize that you deserve to be treated well. It will take some effort, but when you practice thinking and acting in ways that put yourself first, over time you'll find it easier to set limits with others, and that includes the controlling perfectionist.

One way that you can begin to value yourself is by setting aside time each day to do something that *you* want to do, something that's just for you. It doesn't have to be something complicated; in fact, simple activities are often best, because they can be done more easily. Following are some suggestions:

- Read the newpaper or a magazine.

- Exercise or take a walk.

- On your way to work, stop for coffee, tea, or even breakfast.

- Meditate.

- Look into taking a class on a subject you want to learn more about.

- Watch whatever you want to on TV.

- Take time out to do something that you like or enjoy.

Spending time on your own, engaged in an activity that you find invigorating or relaxing, helps you attach importance to yourself and to doing things that benefit you and you alone. If you're used to constantly doing things that benefit others or that others want you to do, this practice may seem strange at first. But the more you do it, the more you'll see that putting your own needs and desires first, even for only a short time each day, can help you learn to care for yourself when faced with many or difficult demands. Soon you'll wonder how you ever got along before you started taking a little time for yourself!

## EXERCISE: Ways to Value Yourself and Boost Your Self-Worth

Think of some activities that you can do to take time for yourself. Remember, these should be simple things you enjoy or that help you charge your batteries, 100 percent solo. Don't include activities that involve or are meant for the benefit of others. Try to come up with at least five things and list them below:

1. _____

2. _____

3. _____

4. _____

5. _____

In *Better Boundaries: Owning and Treasuring Your Own Life*, Jan Black and Greg Enns (1997) list some additional ways that people can develop better self-worth. Following are adaptations of some of their suggestions. Check off at least three that you feel you can commit to on an ongoing basis, in service of yourself.

_____ Make choices that are about *you*.

_____ Be mindful of defeatist statements that you make to yourself (for example: *I can't do anything right. I'm such a screwup*). Once you're aware of these thoughts, consciously stop yourself and substitute a positive statement (*Hey, everyone makes mistakes—why should I be different?*).

_____ Acknowledge your fears and things that cause you anxiety...but then try to challenge these fears. For example, if you get anxious talking to people you don't know, consider saying hello to a stranger every day.

_____ Acknowledge your own preferences—whether in foods, leisure activities, movies, artistic interests, or books—and indulge them.

_____ Decorate your living or work space in ways that you find pleasing and that help assert that this is *your* space. For instance, use photos and pictures that relate to you or your tastes.

_____ When you're having a difficult time making decisions, pretend that it's not you but a friend of yours who's in your situation. Determine what advice you'd offer your friend, and then take it yourself.

_____ Visualize your goals. Where would you like to be a month from now, three months from now, six months, or a year?

..................................................................................

# You Have Rights!

If you've been dealing with a controlling perfectionist for any appreciable length of time, it's easy to feel that you and your views don't count or don't matter. All too often, those close to a perfectionist begin to buy in to the idea that this person really does have all the answers and therefore everyone should submit to his or her view of the world. What's implied, however, is that you have few or no rights. One of the starting points for setting limits and boundaries is being able to accept that you have rights too. Because controlling perfectionists are so often outwardly disciplined and conscientious, it's easy to be impressed by their persistence and goal-directed behavior. Yet often their excessive conscientiousness or devotion to work gets in the way of actually completing tasks and being able to work well with others. In an intimate relationship, the controlling perfectionist may be able at the drop of a hat to criticize a comment you made but have difficulty expressing warm, loving feelings toward you. Therefore this person is, as we all are, imperfect, with no more rights than anyone else.

..................................................................................

# EXERCISE: Declaring Your Rights

One way to set boundaries and limits on perfectionistic and controlling behavior is by identifying those behaviors that you're no longer willing to tolerate and writing a statement or declaration to that effect. Putting something in writing instead of just holding it in your mind can be validating and help you commit to your intentions. And reviewing this document a week from now, a month from now, or a year from now can give you a sense of pride, help you stay on track, or get you back on track.

You can use the template below. Please note that we've purposely left a few of the rights blank, for you to fill in. Here are some examples of the types of rights our clients have expressed: "The right to not be bullied by my boss or coworker"; "The right to not be criticized by my boyfriend"; "The right to be treated respectfully by my wife"; "The right to define my own strengths and weaknesses, not to be defined by my supervisor." You can fill in the blanks with something specific to the rights you wish to assert. In the second part of the declaration, you might use something like "getting baited into arguments" as a behavior you'll no longer put up with and "not overreacting when spoken to in a critical way" as a response. You can revisit and revise this declaration after you finish the book, if you like.

I, _____, being of sound mind and body, do hereby declare that I have the following rights:

The right to be treated with respect.

The right not to be yelled at or demeaned.

The right to refuse to do something that I really don't want to do.

The right not to be bullied into submission.

The right to set my own schedule and agenda and to take things at my own pace.

The right to make mistakes. Making mistakes can be a valuable learning tool.

The right to _____.

The right to _____.

Above all, I have the right to be imperfect!

In accordance with these rights, I swear that I will no longer tolerate or put up with the following behaviors: _____

_____

_____.

In instances in which I encounter these behaviors, I will respond by:

_____ .

................................................................................

Jan Black and Greg Enns (1997) make the point that learning to set effective boundaries is more than a matter of learning general techniques or catchy rules of thumb, because boundary setting must be based on your own beliefs about how you should be treated. If you feel that you have rights and that you deserve to be treated with respect and dignity, you're already of the mind to set better boundaries, especially in stopping patterns of behavior in which you may be treated abusively or dismissively.

# Three Keys to Better Boundaries

Take a minute to think of the types of situations in which the con-trolling perfectionist in your life does things that really bother or annoy you. For instance, you might find any of the following highly offensive:

- Unflattering comments about your appearance

- Comments that belittle your intellect or your interests

- Unrealistic demands, such as asking you to accomplish tasks that you can't possibly finish in the time you have, no matter how hard you work

- Unreasonable demands, such as expecting you to work late or on your days off

- Know-it-all behavior meant to put you down

- Jokes made at your expense

- Overfocus on details to the point of losing sight of the task or discussion at hand

- Insensitivity to your needs

- Disregard for or dismissiveness of your opinions and feelings

- Difficulty expressing warm or loving feelings

In order to set boundaries, it's important that you begin to think of ways you can react to these situations that are different from the way you may usually react. You may have heard the saying "If you want to *feel* something you've never felt before, you must be willing to *do* something you've never done before." Although there are many and various ways to cope with a controlling perfectionist, what we're asking you to consider is whether you're willing to try some new things.

As described earlier, controlling perfectionists are known for demanding that those who work with them or for them do everything perfectly and that they accomplish tasks to those perfectionistic expectations. What most of our clients complain of when dealing with controlling perfectionists is that they find themselves frustrated and exasperated or feeling incompetent or inferior because there's absolutely no way that they can live up to those demands, which may be outrageous to begin with. Often in situations like this they find themselves avoiding conflict by repressing what they really want to say (which may be along the lines of "Will you just shut up for once and let me do things the way I want to?!") or bottling up their feelings—which can be very stressful—because they feel that they don't have the right to say anything to the perfectionist. It's not uncommon for people who keep their feelings bottled up in this way to feel more and more displeased, eventually reaching a point where they explode, launching into a tirade and ending up feeling either guilty or anxious about reprisal. Neither bottling up nor blowing up is a very good place to be, and either situation leads to feeling stressed. This is one of the reasons that those who live or work with a controlling perfectionist often feel a lot of rage (and are therefore more likely to blow up or respond in excess of what the situation calls for) or feel depressed or shut down emotionally—because they don't regularly express how they feel.

So how do you keep from going down this road? How do you put a stop to the "bottling operation" and the situations that provoke it?

You'll need to learn three keys to setting boundaries with a controlling perfectionist and keep them in mind at all times.

1. Don't expect the controlling perfectionist to change or to recognize your talents.

2. Set your own expectations and benchmarks.

3. Although it's important to be assertive, there may be times when it's better to bide your time and wait for the right opportunity to make a statement of your rights.

## Moderate Your Expectations of Change

One of the confusing things about controlling perfectionists is that every so often, they will throw you a bone, which could take the form of a compliment or a statement of gratitude for something you did. But don't be fooled. Controlling perfectionists are even less likely to change spontaneously than they are to change in response to requests to do so (as discussed in chapter 4). Don't imagine that a few kind words mean that the controlling perfectionist has finally recognized your worth or value. Controlling perfectionists may recognize when their behavior has crossed a line, at which point they may provide some grudging praise or words of thanks. Or their momentary approval may be meant to encourage you and keep you on the path to that elusive goal of perfection. They soon are back to their usual ways. So our recommendation is simple: be realistic.

# Set Your Own Expectations and Benchmarks

You know that you're always going to fall short of the controlling perfectionist's expectations. If you try to live up to them, you end up feeling inferior or incompetent, right? So here's the alternative: set your own expectations, goals, and benchmarks. Whether it be at work or at home, in romantic relationships or in friendships, you'll be better off if you try to do the best you can, rather than what the controlling perfectionist wants you to do.

*Jim, a middle school teacher, enjoys his job and likes the interaction he has with his students. Many people consider him a dedicated teacher, and his students' parents know they can count on him to be available if there's some problem or conflict. Unfortunately, Jim's principal, Mrs. Talbot, doesn't share these views of him. She's extremely critical of Jim: she feels that he coddles his students and is too lenient. She implies that Jim is lazy because he doesn't aspire to a supervisory position—however, Jim knows that if he were to be promoted, he wouldn't have as much interaction with students and would become a slave to paperwork. Mrs. Talbot is very vocal about her criticisms of Jim, and it seems as if she tries to make him miserable by micromanaging him—reviewing his lesson plans on nearly a daily basis and making certain he's on time for meetings and lunchroom monitor duty.*

If Jim buys in to Mrs. Talbot's perception of his performance as a teacher, he'll end up feeling incompetent and demoralized. However, if Jim were to measure his value and worth as a teacher based on how his students respond to him, parents' comments that they appreciate his accessibility and fairness, and the fact that he enjoys his work, then by all standards we'd say that Jim is successful. In Mrs. Talbot's opinion, all teachers should aspire to supervisory positions and if they don't there must be something wrong with them. After all, Mrs. Talbot probably feels that everyone should be just like she is...cold, demanding, and critical.

# Know When to Be Assertive and When to Avoid Conflict

Conflicts and disagreements with a controlling perfectionist may often put you in the proverbial "no-win" situation, because even if you're right you'll end up being wronged in the long run: while no one really likes to be proven wrong or incorrect, controlling perfectionists tend to take it as a major attack on their character and retaliate harshly. When you're used to getting that kind of reaction, you may feel that most times it's just not worth it to challenge the controlling perfectionist. While that may be true, avoiding conflict doesn't require that you cave in or let this person walk all over you. For example, to save your energy, rather than react or respond to unreasonable demands you have the option of simply ignoring them (Bernstein 2001). However, it's important for your self-esteem that you be able to express your thoughts and feelings (note that this is not the same as trying to win an argument or persuade the controlling perfectionist to change).

How do you decide when it's in your best interest to speak up? There are no hard and fast rules for when to express yourself versus when to refrain from a confrontation, but it's a good idea to respond any time you're under verbal attack or faced with an unreasonable request. Basic assertive communication skills (discussed in chapter 6) are helpful in any circumstance; however, with a controlling perfectionist you may not get the same response that you would from a more reasonable person. Remember, controlling perfectionists are not known for their sense of empathy and compassion, so don't count on them to respond appropriately to your feelings. Remember, too, that the goal is to establish better boundaries, which sometimes will mean that you need to refrain from buying in to the way in which the controlling perfectionist has defined you. Thus you may need to be somewhat standoffish. However, you should avoid being argumentative—this includes responding angrily or with sarcasm.

The goal of responding assertively to the controlling perfectionist is to put a stop to demanding or what can be abusive behavior without opening yourself up to retaliation. It's very much like walking a tightrope. The following examples illustrate how an assertive response, in contrast with other types of responses, can effectively set boundaries and limits. Although you may be accustomed to using an angry, sarcastic, neutral, or acquiescing response, can you see yourself responding assertively in similar situations? Would an assertive type of response work with the controlling perfectionist in your life? (We discuss assertive communication and assertive responses in more detail in chapter 6.)

**Example 1.** While driving alone, you've had an accident. The car is damaged, but you're okay. Your spouse says: "I can't believe you smashed the car up. I bet you were texting and speeding, right?"

> **Angry/sarcastic response:** "Like you've never had an accident before? *You* drive like a ninety-year-old. And I wasn't texting or speeding. Do you think I enjoy being in car accidents? Oh, and by the way, I wasn't injured, thank God. I know how concerned you'd be about my well-being."

> **Neutral/acquiescing response:** "Yes, I was really upset by the accident too."

> **Assertive response:** "I'm sorry the car was dented. It wasn't my intention to upset you."

**Example 2.** You've made an error when billing a major client. Your boss shouts: "You totally screwed up that client's account. This mistake is going to cost us thousands! What were you thinking?"

> **Angry/sarcastic response:** "Well, I obviously wasn't thinking about the account that much, was I? It must be so comforting to know you're perfect in every way."

> **Neutral/acquiescing response:** "I'm upset also. I didn't mean to make a costly mistake."

**Assertive response:** "I'm sorry about the mistake. I'd like to go over the figures to see where the mistake may have taken place."

**Example 3.** Because of numerous other work responsibilities and priorities, you didn't have time to finish a couple of reports this week. Your supervisor says: "I hope you didn't make any plans for the weekend. You need to come into the office and get these reports done."

**Angry/sarcastic response:** "Wow, that's great! I'd planned to go to the beach, but I'll just bring my boyfriend and some margaritas with me."

**Neutral/acquiescing response:** "I'll change my plans around so I can come in. What time do you want me to be here?"

**Assertive response:** "I know the reports are important, but I wish you'd given me a heads-up so I could have arranged my schedule to complete the reports during the week."

.........................................................................................

# EXERCISE: Assertive Boundary Setting

Practice responding to the following demands in a way that stands up for you and your rights without being oppositional. Once you get good at figuring out assertive responses, you'll write your own alternative responses (angry/sarcastic and neutral/acquiescing), to help you identify such responses as poor choices when the urge to respond in either of these ways arises.

1.  "This house is a mess. Can't you take a few minutes and straighten up? I'm tired of your living like a slob."

    **Angry/sarcastic response:** "It's good that after all these years, you've decided that you don't want to live like a slob!"

    **Neutral/acquiescing response:** "The place does look pretty messy."

**Assertive response:** _____

_____.

2. "I want these expense accounts completed by Wednesday, and don't give me any excuses for why they can't be done by then."

**Angry/sarcastic response:** "Did I happen to mention that the dog ate the expense accounts?"

**Neutral/acquiescing response:** "I'll start to work on them now."

**Assertive response:** _____

_____.

3. "You're always late for our dates. Why can't you just get here on time for once—is that too much to ask?"

**Angry/sarcastic response:** _____

_____.

**Neutral/acquiescing response:** _____

_____.

**Assertive response:** _____

_____.

# A Final Recommendation: Give Yourself Time to Think

Sometimes an unreasonable demand or request may blindside you or make you feel as if you're being put on the spot. This can be one of the most frustrating things about working with or living with a controlling perfectionist. One of our graduate students who had worked in the corporate world for several years reported that her solution to being put on the spot by a boss or administrator was to respond simply, "Let me get back to you on that." She found that this allowed her time to decide what she wanted to say and what approach to use. So if you don't know how to respond in the moment in a way that asserts your rights, stall. It's a useful technique that will most certainly help you at first, until you become practiced in setting limits and boundaries.

As Sandy Hotchkiss (2002) points out, the operative word when setting boundaries is "control," meaning that you stay in control. Remember, controlling perfectionists are accustomed to being in control and getting others to jump when they say so. Although it may seem somewhat unusual for you to take control and set boundaries at first, soon you'll wonder why you let this situation go on for so long. So give yourself permission to respond in new ways to the controlling perfectionist in your life, and practice!

When you assert your *rights*, at the very least the perfectionist may respect your willingness to stick up for yourself, and you set the stage for asking for your *needs* to be met. In the next chapter we talk more about getting the controlling perfectionist to hear you and how to get your point across when advocating for your needs and wishes—here assertive communication can help you again.

# CHAPTER 6

..........................................

# Establishing Better Communication

If you've ever had the experience of trying to communicate honestly and directly with a controlling perfectionist, you've most likely walked away from the encounter thinking, *I may as well have been talking to the wall.* Controlling perfectionists often feel that they know more than anyone else, they're right and anyone who disagrees with them is wrong, or they've cornered the market on what's appropriate or morally correct. So they're usually not interested in listening to others' viewpoints, opinions, or objections or in having any kind of meaningful dialogue. This leaves you feeling as if the controlling perfectionist talks *at* you rather than *with* you. You may feel as if you'd have to beat this person over the head to truly get his or her attention.

Particularly in group settings, the concept that a dissenting view can add value to a discussion is alien to controlling perfectionists. They may pick apart another person's proposal or dominate the discussion in order to bring everyone around to their way of thinking. Short of demanding that others fall in line with their views, they may try to make them feel intimidated into doing so by displaying their wealth of knowledge. So here's the conundrum you may be in: How do you have any kind of meaningful communication with someone who seems to be uninterested in what you have to say, to be incapable of admitting to possibly being wrong, and to feel the need to constantly be in control of situations and people?

In this chapter we offer you many answers to this question. You may need to experiment to see what works and what doesn't work for you. Also, you may find that a particular communication strategy works better with certain people. For instance, something that works fine with your boss may not work with your coworker.

# The Third Way: Moving Toward the Controlling Perfectionist

Let's explore a way of thinking about interpersonal communication that you may find helpful. In any relationship, you have three ways to handle disagreement or conflict: you can choose to move away from, move against, or move toward the other person. (This terminology was coined by the famous psychoanalyst Karen Horney [1937] to describe various personality styles of relating.) When you move away from, you cut down on communication: you avoid the other person, limit contact, or limit conversation length or topics. This was described in chapter 4 as creating space, something you can do to reduce the negative impact of the controlling perfectionist in your life. When you move against, you choose to "do battle" with the other person, defending what you believe, for example, is fair and right. Recommendations for conducting these types of interactions were also given in chapter 4. Whenever you can't or don't want to move away, and moving against isn't likely to have the desired outcome (as is often the case when dealing with a controlling perfectionist), you should try to move toward the other person. This means you neither avoid nor antagonize. The techniques in this chapter will illuminate this third way, which will improve your interactions with the controlling perfectionist and help you communicate effectively.

# Assertive Communication 101

A challenge is how to move toward the other person when you're feeling angry or frustrated. This is where assertiveness comes in handy. The alternative to responding aggressively (blowing up) or passively (bottling up) when your feelings run high in a conflict situation is to simply state how you feel. Here's the basic format for responding assertively: First identify exactly what it is that you're feeling in the situation. Then convey your feeling in a statement beginning with "I feel" that also identifies what the other person did that led you to feel this way: "I feel _____ when you _____." You don't have to explain why you feel this way or justify your feelings, because feelings are neither right nor wrong; they're simply your internal experience.

As an example, let's say someone makes a critical remark about you in front of your friends or family. The remark upsets you greatly, but rather than either bottling up your feelings (for example, not saying anything) or exploding (for example, calling the other person names), you say, "I feel insulted and humiliated when you put me down like that."

After making an assertive statement, stick to your guns—in other words, once you've taken a position, don't back down. Don't apologize for getting upset, concede a minor point, or allow your statement to be picked apart. Examine how you feel afterward. If you've been successful in making a good assertive statement, you won't be fuming (as you might if you bottled up your feeling), nor will you feel guilty for having simply stated how you feel. In a similar situation, make the same statement again.

The next time you're tossing and turning in your bed replaying an argument in your mind and thinking, *I should have said...*, think of an assertive statement you could have used in which you hit the mark and neither bottled up your feelings nor blew up at the other person.

# Assertive Communication with Controlling Perfectionists

Basic assertive communication, while helpful in most situations, may not always work well with controlling perfectionists. Often when you confront controlling perfectionists directly, either they'll become defensive or they'll become just as angry as if you'd blown up at them and lash out at you. The reason is that controlling perfectionists often perceive a clear and direct assertive statement as an assault on their knowledge or intellect. Remember, for controlling perfectionists being right or adhering to rules is paramount to feeling as though they're worthy, so to question their view or authority becomes an attack on the core of their existence. It's also likely that controlling perfectionists will dismiss anything you have to say or argue with whatever point you're trying to get across to them.

Here are some basic rules for communicating assertively with a controlling perfectionist:

1. Don't argue facts, even if you know this person to be wrong. Your energy will be better spent expressing your views, opinions, and feelings. Debating facts may only antagonize a controlling perfectionist.

2. Don't assert that you're right. Soften the blow; preface your statements with phrases like "This is what I was told," "Things may not be always be black or white, but my opinion is," and "I may be wrong, but this is my opinion." This person is more likely to listen to what you say if it doesn't sound like a challenge.

3. Try to stick to one or two basic points and don't stray too far from the main point you want to make.

4. Don't expect this person to hear or validate your feelings. (Note that expressing your feelings is nonetheless important.)

5. Agree to disagree. You may not reach consensus, so it's best to hold your ground with the understanding that you're not going to reach agreement.

6. Be prepared to reiterate the point you're trying to make several times, maybe in different ways, in order to be heard.

When making assertive statements to a controlling perfectionist, try to use kid gloves. Use what you've learned about controlling perfectionists, be sensitive to what makes them different, and avoid setting off this person's perfectionistic and controlling tendencies and traits. Choose your words carefully. Don't create a dead end that makes it easy for this person to turn to criticizing you; show that you acknowledge his or her wants, needs, or feelings and redirect the conversation toward some constructive action to be taken next. Be helpful and guiding.

This may seem like a lot of work, but it gives you the best chance of shaping more considerate or empathic responses in the controlling perfectionist. At the very least, it will help you be heard. In each of the following situations we illustrate how you can take an assertive response that might work well with most people and modify it for use with a controlling perfectionist.

**Situation 1 (at home).** "I can't believe you forgot to pick up my jacket at the dry cleaners, you idiot. Now what am I supposed to wear to work?"

> **Assertive response:** "I really resent your calling me names. Perhaps you should pick up your own dry cleaning. I'd prefer not to have the responsibility."

> **Modified assertive response:** "I'm sorry I forgot to pick up your dry cleaning—that was my mistake. I was really overwhelmed with things I had to do today, and it slipped my mind. Let's see whether we can find you something else to wear. Let's also try to work out a better schedule for who picks up the dry cleaning."

**Situation 2 (at work).** "I know this is last minute, but I need you to stay late and finish up the Jones file."

> **Assertive response:** "I resent your making this request at the last minute. I already have plans for this evening, and it's not convenient for me to stay late."

> **Modified assertive response:** "I see the dilemma you're in about getting the Jones file completed. Unfortunately, I have a prior commitment this evening, and I can't get out of it. Perhaps I can come in early tomorrow and we can work on the file then?"

**Situation 3 (at work).** "I don't care if you're busy right now. Go get me a cup of coffee."

> **Assertive response:** "I dislike being given tasks that aren't part of my job description."

> **Modified assertive response:** "I know how busy you are right now. I have a lot of work to do as well, which I know is important to you. Which task would you rather I do?"

.....................................................................................

# EXERCISE: Practicing Assertive Communication

Decide how you might respond assertively in the following situations. If you want, you can start with a general assertive response and then consider how you might tailor it to a controlling perfectionist.

**Situation 1 (at home).** "I know I agreed to go to the movies with you, but I'm too tired to go to out. I'd rather read the paper and watch TV."

**Your response:** _____

**Situation 2 (at home).** "I'm tired of cleaning up your messes. Can't you do anything right?"

**Your response:** _____

**Situation 3 (at work).** "I'm doing all the work around here—I can't believe I have to work with such lazy, shiftless people like you."

**Your response:** _____

**Situation 4 (at work).** "Why haven't you completed all of the tasks on the list I gave you?"

**Your response:** _____

. . . . . . . . . . . . . . . . . . . . . . . . . . . . . . . . . . . . . . . . . . . . . . . . . . . . . . . . . . . . . . . .

# Defusing the Situation

Different situations call for different responses. In some instances, assertive statements are best. But in other situations you may find that expressing appreciation to a controlling perfectionist or acknowledging this person's strengths while refusing to enter into a discussion of right and wrong can both empower you and allow him or her to back down gracefully. In this way you can keep sight of your own goals for the interaction. You may even get creative and use a bit of humor or dry wit to refrain from taking the bait that controlling perfectionists are so good at dangling in front of you.

> Even though Mary isn't the chairperson of your school committee, she tends to dominate discussions and tries to make decisions for the group. Other committee members have expressed frustration with the way Mary dominates the committee and shuts everyone else down. At a meeting, Mary once again takes control by telling everyone, "Other school districts are doing this type of fund-raiser, and therefore we should do the same—end of discussion."

Any of the following responses might defuse the situation:

• "Mary, I'm glad to see you've done your homework on this, but let's hear other fund-raiser alternatives from the group before we make a decision together."

- "Mary, thanks for your input, but because this is a committee, I think it's important that we all weigh in before coming to a collective decision."

- "I really appreciate your checking out what other districts are doing, and let's keep that alternative in mind as we look at other fund-raising approaches we might consider."

*Ted, your coworker in a civil engineering consulting firm, is constantly correcting everyone's spelling and grammar. You need him to review a report you've written, but he's getting hung up on correcting your English and not spending enough time looking at the more important aspects of the report.*

- "Ted, thanks for correcting my grammar on the report. Now could you look over my calculations also? That's what I'd really like your help with."

- "Ted, it's so comforting to know you're here to help us with the grammar and spelling on our reports."

- "Ted, you're like a frustrated fifth-grade teacher. I think you missed your calling."

Although there are no hard and fast rules for when to use assertive communication versus defusing strategies, defusing strategies may be highly effective or at least preferable with any of the following controlling perfectionists:

- One who's known for being unreasonable and always needs to get the last word in

- One who's particularly vitriolic and vindictive

- One who's known to be explosive

- One who's likely, in front of an audience, to further humiliate you rather than hear what you have to say

# Collaborative Communication

Another strategy you might try is the principle of collaborative communication, in which you try to put your differences aside in order to find what you can agree on. Collaborative communication would advocate that you approach your interactions with the controlling perfectionist in your life with a mind-set of trying to reach collaborative agreements on problems that come up. Rather than being of a win-lose spirit, try to come up with win-win solutions to problematic communication. Here are the three "C"s of collaborative communication:

**Case:** State your case or simply state what your view of the situation or problem is.

**Clarification:** Ask or invite the other person to fully explain his or her view or opinion, so that you're crystal clear on it.

**Commit:** Once both cases or points of view are discussed and clarified, come up with a solution or agreement that you're both willing to commit to...even if it's that you agree to disagree on that particular point or problem.

# Staying in the Adult Role

Some years ago, a book called *I'm Okay—You're Okay* (Harris 1967) became the handbook for a theory known as transactional analysis (TA). According to TA, we all possess three ego states: the Parent, the Adult, and the Child. When a person makes critical remarks about you, this person may be acting in the Parent role; however, you can choose to respond in a manner consistent with your own inner Parent, your inner Adult, or your inner Child. When Mary demands that your school committee do what she feels is the correct thing to do, for example, if you were to respond as the Parent you'd probably hurl a critical remark back at her (for example, "Mary, you're such a bully"), whereas if you were to respond as the Child, you might throw a tantrum—lose control, yelling and screaming—or sulk. In the Adult role, however, you'd take Mary's remarks in stride (as you would when defusing the situation). The optimal kind of communication according to TA is Adult-to-Adult; however, controlling perfectionists tend to manifest either the harsh, critical Parent or the petulant, demanding Child. Therefore achieving optimal communication with a controlling perfectionist may be difficult if not impossible, but you'll create the most conducive situation if you to remember to stay in the Adult role regardless of how this person approaches you. Following are some techniques to help you do so.

## *Sound Bites*

An important part of communicating effectively with controlling perfectionists involves modeling appropriate behavior and responses. Here we describe an approach in which you attempt to shape more positive, empathic behavior and try to speak to the heart of what a controlling perfectionist really wants from you: your approval or admiration. Try to use the following sound bites in various situations with the controlling perfectionist in your life. These stock phrases may be especially useful when the controlling perfectionist has tried to be thoughtful, considerate, or generous, because those are the types of behavior you want to reinforce or acknowledge in some way.

- "I really appreciate it when you take my feelings into consideration."

- "You really can be very caring and considerate when you put your mind to it."

- "Although you have a lot of talents, you also have the ability to relate well to a variety of people."

- "I really appreciate when you compliment me or acknowledge my work."

- "It's really nice that you can be so thoughtful and generous."

# Hit-and-Run Communication

As alluded to earlier, you want to avoid getting into arguments or debates with a controlling perfectionist because, even when you're right, you often end up on the losing end of things. What you may consider when trying to make a point is what we call hit-and-run communication: state precisely what it is that you want to say and then either leave the room or make a quick excuse to end the conversation, like "Sorry, I've got to run. Talk to you later." Don't give the other person time to respond. Your dropping out of the conversation means the other person doesn't have the chance to get defensive or go on the counterattack, as controlling perfectionists often do. The other person feels less confronted, emotions aren't likely to escalate, and your words will sink in better. Here are some examples.

- "I know your mind is made up about what you concluded is the right thing to do, but I just want you to consider my point of view."

- "I was thinking about our plans for the holidays, and I know how committed you are to going to your mother's. I was thinking I'd go to my parents' for the weekend instead."

- "I know you seem dead set against my proposal. The one thing I ask is that you please keep an open mind and give some consideration to my ideas."

Remember, make your statement and then walk away; don't engage in any further discussion until later, after the controlling perfectionist has had time to consider your point or alternative.

# Dealing with Tirades and Temper Tantrums

Although most controlling perfectionists tend to be pretty closed off to expressing feelings, some will attempt to control others through temper tantrums. It's not uncommon to find this type of behavior, especially when a controlling perfectionist feels cornered or fears that some mistake or inadequacy will be uncovered. In those situations, you can expect the controlling perfectionist to launch into a tirade as a means of deflecting blame.

## Sleeping with the Enemy

In the 1991 movie *Sleeping with the Enemy*, Laura Burney (Julia Roberts) is the obedient spouse who goes to great lengths to avoid being physically and verbally abused by her husband (Peter Bergin), making certain that everything is "just so" according to her husband's perfectionistic standards. For instance, she straightens the glasses and cups on the shelves so they're in perfect alignment and she makes sure the house is spotless. The husband is a controlling perfectionist of an extreme yet real sort: one whose methods include physical abuse, threats, or physical intimidation.

If you find yourself in a situation in which you're subject to physical abuse, violence, or threats of physical abuse, seek counseling immediately from an agency that deals with domestic violence or intimate partner violence. We can't emphasize too strongly that the best course of action is to seek professional counseling. Another noteworthy point is that in years of clinical experience in working with batterers, we've yet to come across a batterer who wasn't a controlling perfectionist, a narcissist, or both.

Below is a list of recommendations for dealing with perfectionistic rage and tantrums. These techniques, some of which are adapted from Albert J. Bernstein's 2003 book *How to Deal with Emotionally Explosive People*, may help de-escalate the situation and allow anger to dissipate. With a controlling perfectionist who's less prone to tantrums, you'll also be able to use some of the assertive communication skills we spoke about earlier.

- Don't try to appeal to reason by using rational arguments or explanations.

- Don't make threats or challenge the controlling perfectionist.

- Try to understand the angry controlling perfectionist's mind-set. (Remember, as discussed in chapter 1, that you may be dealing with a hurt child, who felt the need to be perfect in order to gain parental love and affection; someone whose anger is due to anxiety about a situation over which he or she has no control; or someone who struggles to feel competent or adequate.)

- Try to understand the controlling perfectionist's agenda. (Is this person trying to achieve dominance over you by bossing you around or bullying you? Is he or she trying to get you to do something you may not want to do?)

- Determine what your goals are. (Are you simply trying to be heard? What needs are you trying to get met?)

- Speak softly.

- Try to come up with a win-win solution.

- Ask for time, or create distance.

This last technique is similar to the old saying "You don't have to attend every fight you're invited to." There are some times (especially with volatile controlling perfectionists) when it may be better to simply walk away from the situation. It's better to pick your battles or to wait for moments in which there may be a better likelihood that the controlling perfectionist will hear you, rather than to respond in haste when this person is in the grip of strong emotions.

Always be mindful that no matter what the circumstance, you don't deserve to be treated abusively or intimidated; although it may seem that the controlling perfectionist's wrath is the result of something you've done, remember that such behavior is often more about the controlling perfectionist's need to defend or protect themselves than it is about you.

We realize that it may be difficult in the heat of the moment to be mindful of both your reactions and the motives of the controlling perfectionist you're attempting to communicate with. It will help if you review the foregoing guidelines any time you're anticipating a contentious interaction with a controlling perfectionist who's prone to tantrums.

# The Need for Repetitive Communication

We want to be careful to not create the impression that better communication will in general put an end to arguments and conflicts with a controlling perfectionist, nor is any single statement you make likely to lead to an "aha moment" in which this person realizes the error of his or her ways. Remember that this person's need for control and perfection is highly ingrained. You'll probably continue to have the same kind of disagreements with the controlling perfectionist over and over again. You may feel in these situations that whatever communication strategy you used last time didn't work, because here you are again.

But the truth is that better communication has a cumulative effect—over time, the character of your interactions will change. You may feel sometimes as if you're repeating yourself, and in fact you should expect to feel this way. Try to reiterate the same points in different ways or using a variety of techniques if you can. For best results, plan which communication strategy you'll use before you approach an interaction rather than try to remember one on the spur of the moment, and don't expect to see immediate results.

*Tina is a scout leader for her twelve-year-old daughter's group. She co-leads the group with Helene, a mother of one of the other girls. Usually, Tina or Helene will arrange to have an activity for the girls to do when they meet each week. Tina is aware that Helene is a control freak when it comes to scheduling meetings and activities; however, she has learned to take things in stride and negotiate dates and times with Helene.*

*The problem that has come up recently is that Helene constantly corrects the girls when they're working on projects—she won't let them work on their own. When the girls were arranging food baskets for a local homeless shelter, Helene jumped in and rearranged all the baskets. The girls just roll their eyes at this sort of behavior, but they've begun to disengage from the activities, so Tina decides it's time to mention this to Helene and ask that she step back to allow the girls to do their own projects. Tina musters the courage to speak with Helene and decides how she'll broach the topic assertively but in a non-accusatory, nonjudgmental way. In spite of Tina's carefully chosen words, Helene jumps down Tina's throat and outright denies that she's being overbearing with the girls. Tina feels as if she can't get through to Helene, and she doesn't know what to do.*

*Tina decides to wait for an opportunity to raise the issue again. At the next meeting, when the girls are working on another community project, Tina says something to Helene. This time, Helene backs off and angrily tells the girls, "I'm not helping any of you; go ahead and make your own mistakes." The girls look confused, but Tina knows that Helene is now in passive-aggressive mode—if Helene can't do it her way, she won't do it at all. Tina sees the change in Helene's response as something positive, however, and plans her next step: when the time is right she tells Helene that she appreciates her helping with the girls' projects but that both of them need to let the girls take ownership of their work in order to keep them engaged in the meetings. Helene is still entrenched in her denial but is willing to heed Tina's suggestion.*

# Responding to Perfectionistic and Controlling Characteristics and Traits

In chapter 1 we described twelve characteristics and traits of controlling perfectionists. We'll now review nine of those traits, identifying the main difficulty with or challenge to communication each trait creates and offering communication strategies similar to the ones we've presented throughout this chapter.

**A need for perfection so great that it interferes with their ability to attain happiness or satisfaction in life**

**Communication challenge.** The controlling perfectionist feels an overwhelming burden to meet impossibly high standards and approaches daily tasks with a great sense of pressure to do everything perfectly. Thus if you challenge or correct the controlling perfectionist on something, this person is likely to become defensive rather than give consideration to your view or opinion.

**Communication strategy.** This is an example of where Adult-to-Adult communication may be helpful. Keep in mind that the controlling perfectionist probably doesn't wake up in the morning wondering how he or she can make your life miserable. Instead of challenging this person, see whether you can reach some type of consensus, or perhaps you can even agree to disagree on something rather than escalate an argument that may end up going nowhere. People don't have to agree on everything. Try saying: "I'll consider your point of view if you'll consider mine. Then let's come back to the subject. What do you think?"

**A preoccupation with rules, lists, organization, and orderliness, to such an extent that they often seem to miss the point of an activity or task**

**Communication challenge.** The controlling perfectionist wants you to be just as preoccupied with rules, lists, organization, and orderliness. You may need to communicate that you may not be as invested in these things and that there's nothing wrong with having differences of opinion as to how things can be accomplished. Alternatively, you may have to communicate in such a way as to keep this person on task and focused on the big picture, otherwise the work may take too long or never be finished. At other times, this person may refuse to recognize or adapt to new and better ways of doing things.

**Communication strategy.** Depending on whether this occurs in your personal or work life, you may want to employ different strategies. For example, you may not be in a position to say to your boss, "I really don't feel like coming into the office every day." However, you may be able to negotiate a way in which you can circumvent the rules and still get the job done. For example, "Would you consider my working from home one or two days a week, provided that I can keep my sales numbers up?" You may ask for clarification of some of the rules or lists that are being imposed: "I have ten tasks I've been given that I'm working on right now. Could you help me prioritize them?" In other types of relationships you may point out that sometimes organization and routine get in the way of spontaneity and fun.

Alternatively, acknowledge that getting drawn into details or sidetracked by a perfectionistic undertaking might be productive or desirable, but remind the controlling perfectionist about your goals. For example:

- "I know you want to reorganize the bookshelves, but we agreed to work on the taxes on Saturday, and I'd like for us to stay focused on that. Are you in agreement?"

- "I appreciate the work you've done on this report, but I think it'd be best to stick to the main point we discussed. We can use the other material for another project."

One of our clients, a respected internist in a group practice, was once told by a perfectionistic and controlling older physician to prescribe a certain medication, but this medication was outdated, having been found ineffective. Our client had to come up with a strategy to convey her discomfort without attacking her superior. She decided to use a collegial approach: "I found some articles on a newer medication, one that I think may be helpful to this particular patient. Could you look them over and let me know what you think before I write the prescription?" This kind of Adult-to-Adult communication worked well in this case.

**A tendency to procrastinate, out of a fear of not doing things right**

**Communication challenge.** You may need to make sure the controlling perfectionist follows through on tasks this person has promised to do or complete.

**Communication strategy.** Get the controlling perfectionist to agree to a time frame or accelerate the process somehow. This is a situation in which direct, assertive communication may be helpful. For example:

- "I know you're working hard on finding the right appliances for the new kitchen. Could we take your top three choices and then we can decide on one of those?"

- "I give you a lot of credit for the work you've put in on the Bronson case. Could you give me the first draft by Monday so we can go over our strategy? We need to wrap this up quickly."

**A need to control the finances, schedules, and other details of the lives of those with whom they're close; moodiness and anxiety when they're not in charge**

**Communication challenge.** Whether the perfectionist tries to control you through overt comments or criticisms or through indirect or more subtle attempts, you may often be in a position of having to assert your right to control your finances, your free time, or your schedule.

**Communication strategy.** Use some of the basic boundary-setting strategies discussed in chapter 5 or some of the basic assertive communication skills we talked about in this chapter. For example: "I'm not happy with the financial arrangement, and I want more of a say in how we spend our money. I don't want to be relegated to a weekly allowance as though I were an irresponsible teenager. Can we discuss this so we can come up with a more equal partnership regarding our finances?"

You may also use the three "C"s of collaborative communication to resolve issues with schedules or time management. Here's what this might look like:

> **Case:** "I agree that we should set aside time on Saturdays to work on the house, and I know how important this is to you. But the Smiths have invited us to go out on their boat this Saturday, and I'd like for us to go with them."
>
> **Clarification:** "Is there any reason we can't postpone the house work until Sunday or next Saturday?"
>
> **Commit:** "All right, so that's the plan: we'll go with the Smiths this Saturday and work on the house both days next weekend."

### Unrealistically high expectations and standards for others' performance and behavior

**Communication challenge.** You may need to convey that while you do share the view that any job worth doing is worth doing well, your standards will naturally differ from those of a perfectionist, and perfectionism places unreasonable demands on others and breeds misery.

**Communication strategy.** Convey that you've tried your best and that you appreciate the input and feedback (read: criticism). Try defusing the situation. For example: "I really appreciate your feedback in pointing out the mistakes I made on the project summary. I'm really learning more about how you'd like these summaries done." We know it may sound disingenuous, but by expressing appreciation, you're moving toward, not away from or against: getting along with the perfectionist as best you can, in a way that honors you both. Even if the controlling perfectionist says something like "Well, your best just isn't good enough," we recommend that you stick to your guns by restating that you truly have tried your best and that you're not attempting to slack off or be disingenuous.

**An excessive devotion to work and productivity, to the point at which they have difficulty having fun or devoting time to friendships**

**Communication challenge.** The controlling perfectionist expects that you share the same devotion to work and that you be willing to sacrifice your free time—for example, working late every day and coming in to work on weekends. You may need to assert your limits or boundaries while at the same time conveying that you're a hardworking, motivated person.

**Communication strategy.** Structure your free time. Schedule events and activities to make even your downtime seem productive and busy. We're not saying that you need to be more active in your nonworking hours, just plan how you'll use them (you can always change your plans later), so that you can assert your right to your own free time by referring to what you've scheduled. This pays tribute to the perfectionist's need for productivity. When necessary, affirm that you're a hardworking team player by collaborating to do extra work at a time that's more convenient for you. Let's say your boss asks you to come in on Saturday morning to finish up some work on a project, but you don't want to miss your son's Little League game. This is a situation in which collaborative communication may be useful. You could say something like "I'd like to be able to come in Saturday, but I have something important already scheduled. I'm willing to come in early or stay late on Monday instead. Could we work on the project then?"

## Stinginess with time or money; miserliness

**Communication challenge.** Trying to get more money out of a controlling perfectionist may feel like trying to get blood out of a stone. Also, because controlling perfectionists are known for being stingy not just in a monetary or financial sense but also when it comes to giving of themselves, you may have a hard time getting information out of them or finding out what they're thinking or feeling. Some people describe such attempts at communication as "like pulling teeth."

**Communication strategy.** Make your needs clear and state exactly what you want. For example, you could use the three "C"s of collaborative communication, as in the following case:

> **Case:** "With the money you've allotted to me in the household checking account, every month I have $300 to buy groceries and other essentials like things we need at the pharmacy, but every month we run over. If we don't agree to come up with a more reasonable amount for these expenses, we'll just have to do without certain luxuries."
>
> **Clarification:** "Do you understand what I'm asking? What are your thoughts?"
>
> **Commit:** "Okay, let's both commit to making that amount work."

As a reminder, you may need to be persistent and repetitive in your attempts at communicating your case.

## A reluctance to delegate tasks to others; an attitude of "If you want something done right, do it yourself"

**Communication challenge.** You may need to communicate that you're up to the challenge of handling work delegated to you and that your goal is to work collaboratively, both so that you can make valuable contributions and so that the controlling perfectionist isn't overworked.

**Communication strategy.** Convince the controlling perfectionist that you're capable of handling the task and yet willing to allow this person to feel somewhat in control of the way in which you do it. In this situation, sound bites and hit-and-run communication may be useful. For example:

- "You're trying to do everything. I don't know how you do it all. Let me take over some of the burden. I promise I'll follow your instructions and will check in with you if I'm uncertain how you'd handle a particular situation. Tell you what—think it over and then let's talk about it."

- "I know I can handle balancing the checking account. Let me try it this month and then we can go over it. Please just think about it!"

It may be difficult for the controlling perfectionist to hand over control, but your persistence may pay off in the long run, with this person being more willing to let you and others have responsibility.

**Difficulty both expressing feelings and identifying others' feelings, as if cut off from emotional life; a cold and cheerless exterior**

**Communication challenge.** Engaging in a discussion of your feelings and then trying to find out what the controlling perfectionist is feeling may be somewhat like talking with someone who speaks a different language.

**Communication strategy.** Try to elicit or draw out how the controlling perfectionist is feeling or may be reacting to what you've said or to a particular situation. Here it may work best to follow principles of assertive communication and begin by saying how you're feeling or guessing at what the controlling perfectionist is feeling. If you need to find out how this person is feeling in order to move forward with a decision, for example, you might say:

- "I'm not sure about your reactions to the estimate we've been given to remodel the kitchen. Could you let me know your thoughts and feelings on this so we can make a decision?"

- "I'm not sure how you feel about going to your cousin's wedding. You haven't said anything, but I sense some discomfort. Could you tell me what your thoughts and feelings are about the invitation?"

- "I get the feeling that you're fuming over last month's credit card statement, but you haven't said anything. Could we talk about this so that we can come up with a plan for how to pay down the bill?"

It may be hard to get a controlling perfectionist to express feelings, if you convey that you're truly interested in this person's reactions and emotions, eventually your efforts may pay off.

# Keeping Track of Your Communication Style

Sometimes when you attempt to change a behavior, it's helpful to keep a journal or a log of your progress. This can help you stay focused and also help you determine what's been helpful in certain situations and what hasn't. You can use the format below.

| Situation | My response | Type of response | What I wish I had said |
|---|---|---|---|
|  |  |  |  |

**Situation.** Describe what the controlling perfectionist did to upset you. Did this person make you the target of a critical remark? Did this person put you down in front of friends or family? Was this person especially critical of your work or something you did for him or her? Did this person make some kind of outlandish demand that was beyond your capabilities?

**My response.** Paraphrase your response and note any observations about the way in which you made it. Did you stutter and stammer as you attempted to find your words? Did you speak quietly, or did you shout?

**Type of response.** Given all the types of communication discussed in this chapter, how might you characterize your response? Was it an attempt at collaborative communication, assertive communication, sound bites, or hit-and-run communication? Were you sticking to your guns and repeating something you've said before? Did the strategy you chose seem effective? Or, if you didn't choose a strategy, was this an example of bottling up or blowing up?

**What I wish I had said.** If you had the opportunity to relive the situation, what would you have said and how would you have expressed yourself? What strategy might have worked better?

Following are two example entries.

| Situation | My response | Type of response | What I wish I had said |
|---|---|---|---|
| Friday, April 12: At the end of the day, Dennis (my boss) hollered at me in front of everyone about my not having finished the monthly report, even though it's not due until Tuesday. | I didn't know what to say. I just sort of stood there, stunned. After he left, I didn't say anything; I was just glad to be going home. | Bottling up | I should have taken Dennis aside and said: "I really don't appreciate being yelled at in front of my coworkers. I feel embarrassed and frustrated. I know the report isn't due until Tuesday, so my plan was to come in early on Monday and have it completed in plenty of time for you to review it. Have I been late with monthly reports before?" |

| Tuesday, April 16: Dennis criticized me in the monthly meeting for not including a comparison chart in the report. | I replied immediately and calmly, "I'm surprised you didn't suggest that if you thought it would be helpful." | Assertive communication (It wasn't really effective because he got defensive and went on to express doubts about my judgment and ability.) | I could have defused the situation by saying something like "I appreciate your input, Dennis. Next time I'll consult you before finalizing the report." |

Establishing better communication with the controlling perfectionist in your life may be difficult but not impossible. It does require persistence and patience on your part and a willingness to try out some of the strategies that we've discussed in this chapter. Again, please remember that what may work in one situation may not work in another, so think of these strategies as a tool kit: sometimes you may need to try a screwdriver, while at other times you may need a hammer; whatever you try, keep in mind the experimental nature of your efforts at better communication.

In the next chapter we discuss ways to manage interpersonal relationships with controlling perfectionists who may be among your friends or family members.

......................................

# CHAPTER 7

# Handling Controlling Perfectionists in Romantic Relationships, Family Life, and Friendships

I n this chapter, we cover several problems you'll most likely encounter when involved with a controlling perfectionist, explain how these manifest in different types of relationships, and illustrate how to deal with them effectively. There are a few keys to success here that you should keep in mind.

First, remember that controlling perfectionists are often blind to their problems, as mentioned in the introduction. Although it may be tempting to do so, trying to explain to them that they have a problem they need to fix is unlikely to do you any good. Even if you sense the moment is ripe for you to educate the controlling perfectionist or to argue for change, resist. Concentrate instead on your own behaviors and trying to transform the nature of the relationship rather than the controlling perfectionist.

Second, bear in mind the saying "If you always do what you did, you will always get what you got." To deal better with a controlling perfectionist you'll most likely have to do something different than you've been doing. Many of the strategies offered here might make you feel uncomfortable at first; they'll stretch you at times. Even if you don't "get it right" immediately, don't be too concerned; just be persistent and the changes will eventually pay off.

Finally, be prepared to accept small or no changes at first, and be determined to keep on trying. Stick with the plan and eventually you'll get some results. There might also be some consolation in the idea that even though change isn't coming quickly, you're doing the best you possibly can under the circumstances.

(Note: if you have a perfectionistic and controlling sibling, in this chapter "friendships" probably best describes your relationship.)

# Emotional Constrictiveness and a Lack of Affectionate Expression

Controlling perfectionists feel that they must be in control of their emotions at all times. Losing their cool is anathema to them, because it can lead to improprieties and mistakes. They hold fervently to the idea that everyone should maintain perfect control and be in possession of their sensibilities at all times.

## In Romantic Relationships

The emotional tone that controlling perfectionists seem to prefer is one of polite restraint; this is particularly true regarding public displays of affection. Your perfectionistic and controlling partner may be reluctant to kiss or hold hands when in company or out and about.

This quality considerably manifests itself in sexual relationships. Controlling perfectionists may be giving and attentive lovers because they feel that satisfying their partners' sexual needs is the right thing to do. But they may lack creativity, passion, spontaneity, and adventurousness. Or they may be attentive in areas in which

they feel a good lover should be but not necessarily give their partners what they desire.

In women, the need for self-control and thus the refusal to sur-
render to passion often results in an inability to obtain an orgasm.
Nevertheless, a perfectionistic and controlling woman may continue to perform her sexual "duties," believing that a good wife or
girlfriend should do these types of things regardless of the lack of
pleasure and satisfaction it affords her. She may begin to harbor
resentments, however, due to not getting what she feels she deserves.
Often she won't give voice to this displeasure because, in her mind,
this would make her a bad wife or girlfriend. Thus sex for her
becomes more and more of a chore. Further, her sexual frustration
may boil over into other areas of the relationship.

A perfectionistic and controlling man may believe that his
partner's emotional desires for sexual connectivity and intimacy
are unreasonable. He might, for example, totally ignore foreplay
that includes intimate talking and affectionate touching.
Perfectionistic and controlling men also often don't see the connection between their constant criticism of their partners' imperfections and their partners' lack of sexual desire for them. They're
often blind to the fact that someone who has been carped on all
day long probably won't be sexually available later on.

Sex with a controlling perfectionist is often complicated by
other aspects of his or her perfectionism as well. Due to a fear of
moral transgression—believing that certain sexual acts are evil or
perverted—controlling perfectionists may refuse to explore ways to
enhance their sex life or better satisfy their partners. They might
claim, for example, that oral sex is "unnatural." This is particularly
true of the puritanical compulsive subtype (see chapter 1). Yet
another barrier to sexual intimacy is the fact that many controlling
perfectionists are neat freaks. The natural fluids and odors involved
during lovemaking can be repugnant to a controlling perfectionist.
The need to clean up before and immediately after sex can severely
damage the spontaneity of a good sex life.

Finally, one of the more recent findings about controlling perfectionists is that they're "intimacy phobic," as discussed in chapter
2. A good sex life will often bring couples closer together, and for

exactly this reason controlling perfectionists often avoid sex. Intimacy and a close partnership, to controlling perfectionists, mean giving up a good deal of control. The thought of having to do things their partners' way can be very frightening to controlling perfectionists; they may fear that their partners' needs will overwhelm them. Also, intimacy naturally involves sharing truths and expressing true feelings—here controlling perfectionists feel too vulnerable. As explained in chapter 1, controlling perfectionism is often a means of covering up one's own inadequacies or unacceptable desires, so controlling perfectionists don't want to feel pressure to open up and reveal their secrets. To express who they really are would shatter the facade and subject them to judgment themselves.

## In Family Life

Emotional constrictiveness often expresses itself in controlling perfectionists' attitudes toward their children. Controlling perfectionists are highly reserved and proper when relating to their children. They may, for example, assert that people shouldn't use baby talk with infants and toddlers but rather teach them proper English and grammar. Or they may think that tickling children will just turn them into ridiculously silly humans. They may criticize their children for acting silly or even joyful.

This aversion to the overt expression of emotions may often lead controlling perfectionists to avoid fun family gatherings or to avoid participating in any type of spontaneous play. Rather than partake in such activities, they usually prefer to retreat to the office, the garage, or anyplace else.

> Glenn, a controlling perfectionist who had a wife and three young children, dreaded his days off from work. This was particularly true in the summertime, when his family would drag him to the local water park. He went only because otherwise he'd feel guilty for not spending time with them, yet the whole time he'd sit on the sidelines as his family "splashed around like a bunch of idiots and shrieked like a bunch of wild animals." His harsh criticism of their

*joyful abandon was due to his feeling humiliated at his inability to*
*let down his composure and similarly lose himself in having fun.*

# In Friendships

A controlling perfectionist with whom you share a friendship may constantly tell you to do such things as lower your voice, stop arguing, settle down, and be rational, pointing out just how embarrassing it is for both of you when you lose self-control.

Controlling perfectionists value thought, analysis, and ideas—particularly moralistic or rule-oriented ideas—much more than they do emotions. For example, it wouldn't be unusual for a controlling perfectionist, when watching a particularly emotional part of a movie, to comment on the excellent cinematography and directorial qualities of the scene while you and others in the theater are sobbing helplessly.

It's rare to find a controlling perfectionist who's emotionally engaged with friends, family, and siblings. Controlling perfectionists' relationships tend to be formal in nature. They can be quite dutiful toward their friends and others while still maintaining distance and independence. For sure they'll remember birthdays and other significant events and holidays. They'd never forget to send a birthday greeting or to visit a friend in the hospital and may even meet for lunch from time to time. They may send out periodic e-mails or electronic greeting cards. They might share things they like, such as jokes or links to videos on YouTube, on a regular basis. They might even lend money and offer excellent advice when their friends or family members are in trouble. But they may be quite stingy with their time and insist on not becoming too involved. They may make sure that they have plenty of time in between actual physical contacts and that these contacts are relatively short in duration, allowing them to keep their freedom. They may silently resent being asked to do favors or chores for their friends and loved ones and might even look to get even for it somehow in the future.

# Handling Emotional Constrictiveness and Lack of Affectionate Expression

Bear in mind that controlling perfectionists view an emotional display as a sign of weakness, a loss of self-control. Your insisting that they become more emotional will never work; they'll only harden their resistance and vehemently defend themselves against the unmerited criticism on your part. Most likely you'll have an argument on your hands as they extol the virtues of reason over passion and self-control over wanton emotional abandon. Or, if you're more fortunate, they might admit that they'll never feel the need to be as close as you do and will never be as emotional as you are and that's just the way they are.

To make an emotional connection with the controlling perfectionist in your life, consider looking for and taking advantage of teachable moments in which you have the opportunity to respond positively to a spontaneous and unsolicited show of emotion. You might not feel that the controlling perfectionist is expressing emotion, because it will be a rudimentary effort at best, so be alert to even the most minor of displays. Try to avoid commenting on the fact that this person is actually expressing emotion—statements like "Oh—I see you have feelings" and "I'm so excited over the progress you're making in showing your emotions" usually serve only to embarrass controlling perfectionists. Instead, when these teachable moments occur, be warm, accepting, and a very good listener. A controlling perfectionist who slowly learns that he or she can express a little emotion without being attacked, ridiculed, or made to feel foolish will be much more willing to risk expressing *more* emotion.

Look for progress, not total transformation, and be grateful for small gains. Be willing to go slowly. Finally, bear in mind that even with practice and encouragement, a controlling perfectionist will most likely never be as emotionally expressive as you are.

## Example: Romantic Relationship

*One night Sam was speaking with his perfectionistic and controlling wife, Bela. She and Sam had had a particularly good day, and she'd let down her guard a little because it was late and she was tired. Because Bela's birthday was coming up, Sam asked her what she wanted for her birthday, when suddenly her face saddened. "You know," she said. "The best birthday that I ever had was one on which I never received one single present. I was away at college, and everybody sent me a birthday card with no gifts. But each card was so heartfelt and genuine. I felt so very loved!" Sam recognized that Bela's expressing emotion as she reminisced created a teachable moment. He made a statement how it was nice to have good friends and how important they were, which led to a discussion about how important their friends were in their lives and how much they loved and cared for them. They went on to have a very affectionate night of lovemaking, which was a real breakthrough for them at the time.*

## Example: Family Life/Friendship

*For most of their lives, largely due to their parents' fighting as they were growing up, Jenna had been very protective of her sister, Moira, who was three years her junior. She felt the need to control Moira's every move, giving her a steady stream of advice, mostly of a critical nature. Although a controlling perfectionist, Jenna was very well-meaning insofar as her motives were to protect her younger sister. Even after their parents divorced and Moira came into young adulthood, the nature of this relationship persisted.*

*Moira, however, wanted a more real type of relationship with her sister, one that involved closeness, openness, and intimacy.*

*During one family celebration, the two of them were working together in the kitchen. In a rare moment, Jenna told Moira: "You're a big help. I've always appreciated your willingness to jump in and do your share." Moira, seeing this as a teachable moment, told her sister that she appreciated all of her input and help. Jenna grew tearful; she'd never thought that Moira appreciated her help.*

*The two embraced and promised to do more things together. They*
*began by having weekly lunches in which they celebrated their "new*
*relationship."*

# Control Issues

Controlling perfectionists want to be in control all the time, in
large part due to their lack of confidence in their abilities. Their
lack of genuine self-confidence engenders a constant need to be
seen as capable. They don't like surprises, because events they're
unprepared for shake their sense of control. Furthermore, they
don't trust other people to do anything they could do themselves—if
someone else is in control, there's a fear that this person won't do
things exactly right or to the controlling perfectionist's high standards. Bear in mind that controlling perfectionists feel inadequate,
and only through perfectionism can they feel certain that they're
"getting it right."

## *In Romantic Relationships*

Rather than risk spending too much money by allowing his
wife to purchase a couch, a perfectionistic and controlling husband
will insist on purchasing it himself. Rather than let her husband get
the children ready for school and risk a potentially embarrassing
situation, such as sending their children to school without their
homework—which, for a controlling perfectionist, could be a catastrophe—a perfectionistic and controlling wife will insist on getting
the children ready herself.

*Ryan, a controlling perfectionist, was talking to his psychologist.*
*"I just don't get her," he said. "What wife wouldn't want a new car?*
*And yet, when I bring it home, she's all over my case. It seems that*
*I should have allowed her to choose the kind of car that she wanted.*
*I got her red; she wanted blue. I got a sun roof; she wanted a*
*convertible. I just can't seem to get this right. She tells me I'm*

*controlling, but hey, does she know how to pick out a car? What does she know? She doesn't care about anti-swerve, four-wheel drive if she gets stuck in the snow, and she'd get the stupid stereo package that sounds like crap. Now she's not talking to me. Any other woman would appreciate what I was trying to do for her."*

Ryan failed to understand, as most controlling perfectionists do, that no one likes feeling as if their input is unwelcome, especially in a marriage. Perhaps Ryan *is* better at picking out cars, but it's obvious that his wife would want to have some say. She's more upset with Ryan's consistent need to control her. The marriage most likely has reached the point where material things matter less than doing things together does.

In a partnership or marriage, the need to control usually leads a controlling perfectionist to take on the lion's share of duties and chores. At first you might be overjoyed at the prospect of not having to do some chore that the controlling perfectionist takes off your hands, but be aware that controlling perfectionists will overload themselves, burning the candle at both ends and ramping up their stress levels, as a result becoming even more irritable and critical. Not surprisingly, controlling perfectionists, as mentioned in chapter 2, often battle stress-related disorders, such as chronic headaches, gastrointestinal problems, and back problems. TMJ, a condition due to tension in the jaw, is not uncommon among controlling perfectionists. Additionally, controlling perfectionists are prone to anxiety and mood disorders, such as panic attacks, excessive worrying, and depression.

## In Family Life

*Sarah participated in a party in her daughter's kindergarten classroom where there were a number of structured activities that the parents could do together with their children. Many of these activities were craft oriented. Sarah completed every craft without exception on her own, without her daughter's input, as her daughter just watched. The idea that the activity should be done*

*perfectly was more important to Sarah than was the idea of*
*collaborating on a project and enjoying each other's company.*

As in this example, some parents seem to constantly be doing things for their children that instead they could do *with* their children or their children could do by themselves. These parents tend to hover over their children, trying to control every aspect of their children's lives. Such "helicopter parents" dictate and interfere with their children's activities, friendships, clothing, and academic decisions and just about anything else they feel that they can or should control. They're constant advocates for their children, and when their children are accused of any wrongdoing they rush to defend them, regardless of whether the children might actually be misbehaving or in the wrong. If a child has a disagreement with peers, the helicopter parent will butt in; if the child has problems in the classroom, the helicopter parent will demand satisfaction from the administration, even to the point of moving the child out of a particular teacher's class. Helicopter parents are a growing concern among educators and other professionals who work with children.

Aside from the headaches they cause for other adults, the problem with these parents is that they don't allow children to make their own decisions, stick up for themselves, or accept the consequences of their wrongdoing, thereby robbing them of valuable life experiences. They don't prepare their children to be adults who cope with their own problems; thus these children will have a tendency to always need the type of help that the helicopter parent gives and in fact feel entitled to have things done for them (see for example Honore 2008).

As their children grow up, helicopter parents have been known to actually call their children's employers, decide on roommates for them, and select their colleges and even their spouses. When one young woman began to date at age twenty-two, her perfectionistic and controlling mother insisted on driving her, in spite of the fact that her daughter had her own driver's license. (See Gibbs 2009 for more on helicopter parents, in a Time.com article.)

## In Friendships

Controlling perfectionists would control everything if they had the strength. They feel that they're the only ones who can do things right, whether it's choosing where to go camping, packing the gear and supplies, selecting the route, or driving to the campsite. The obvious problem with this is that *you* don't get to do things. The controlling perfectionist ends up doing everything, leaving you feeling isolated. Opportunities for the two of you to interact through collaboration are sacrificed to the perfectionist's need for control. Sharing, one of the key components in any close relationship, is neglected. Alternatively, when you do things, the controlling perfectionist makes it seem as if you're not up to the task, picks apart your approach, or finds something to complain about later; as a result you feel inferior.

# Handling Control Issues

Probably one of the most important strategies here is to simply speak up and assert your right to control the things that you need to control. It's important that you don't give up control of the things that affect you the most, especially the things the controlling perfectionist can't ultimately control. As we stated in a previous chapter, people can't control the way you behave when you're not with them—for example, unless you work for your parents, your parents can't control what you do when you're at work or with friends. They might tell you that you should do certain things at work or talk to your friends in a certain manner, but of course they can't control what you actually do.

Sometimes you have to take a stand to reinforce this idea. This isn't always easy. Most likely there will always be something extra that you have to do—some cost you have to pay.

## *Example: Romantic Relationship*

*George worked at home, operating a business out of the spare bedroom. His wife, Leia, would continually interfere with his work, often insisting that he leave "the office" to do something for her. George decided to take a stand to assert his right to control his own business. He told Leia that the next time she did that, he'd leave and rent a hotel room for the day so he could accomplish his work. He was good to his word, and though it made Leia furious, over the next few weeks, every time she interfered, he'd follow through with getting a hotel room. Finally, when she realized that he'd stick to his guns no matter what, Leia promised she'd no longer interfere.*

Note in this example that George had to pay a price both in terms of money and in having to contend with his wife's anger. This may seem unfair—you shouldn't have to be the one to make sacrifices—but it's a typical cost of making changes.

## *Example: Family Life*

*Tiara was in tenth grade. Whenever she spoke on her cell phone at home, her father would constantly tell her how to talk to whomever she was speaking with. After many failed attempts to get him to stop, she'd lock herself in her bedroom whenever she spoke on her cell phone. Her father was very angry at first, but when he realized that Tiara wouldn't budge, he soon gave up and she was able to have phone conversations in front of him.*

Where control is an issue, you may find it best to do a lot of things separately. For example, if your spouse continues to control the household spending without your input, you'd do well to create separate checking accounts. If you and your roommate are attending an event for which he insists on arriving a half hour early, and as you go about getting ready he harasses you for fear of being late, you'd do well to take separate cars. Many people don't like doing things separately, because it makes them feel less like a couple, less like family, or less like friends. Yet there will always be some things that you have to do separately in a relationship, especially with a controlling perfectionist. Controlling perfectionists will often complain bitterly at your first attempts to do things separately and then most likely increase their efforts to control you. But if you stick to your guns and don't budge, they'll get used to it.

The "disconnect" when you do things separately may feel threatening to your relationship. However, you can convey your wish to maintain the relationship and even strengthen it by simply "reconnecting" in areas that don't involve control issues. In other words, disconnect in areas in which the other person is trying to control you, and reconnect in other areas. Exactly what these areas are may differ in every relationship—we can't tell you what they'd be for you and the controlling perfectionist in your life—but if you look, you'll find them.

## Example: Romantic Relationship

*Bill couldn't help trying to control how his wife, Catherine, cleaned the house. Whenever she tried to clean with him around, his bossiness made her feel like a servant. One of Bill and Catherine's favorite things to do, on the other hand, was sit down and have a cup of coffee together. So in the mornings before Bill left for work, rather than do any cleaning, Catherine (who stayed at home) would share a cup of coffee and talk with him. She'd wait to clean until later, when he wasn't there to criticize her.*

## Example: Family Life

*Crystal would try to interfere every time Arturo tried to teach the children something, usually some sports skill. She'd constantly tell him what to say to them and correct him if she thought he was wrong. Arturo learned to simply make sure that he taught the children these things when she wasn't around. But he'd also invite her to participate in their roughhousing and playing backyard football.*

# *Example: Friendship*

*Two men, childhood friends named Charlie and Herb, had a monthly ritual of meeting each other for dinner. Both men were reasonably successful and enjoyed good food and wine. However, Charlie, a controlling perfectionist, would continually offer advice on how Herb should treat his wife. Charlie claimed to know best because he knew more about women and also had watched Herb grow up and thus knew what "made him tick." When Herb protested the criticism and unwelcome comments, Charlie told him that he'd just have to "man up" and accept advice once in a while and not be such a baby. After a while, Herb simply canceled the dinners. He told Charlie that he'd be happier if the two of them went to sporting events and movies instead (activities that limited opportunities for conversation).*

..............................................................................................

# *EXERCISE:* Disconnecting and Reconnecting

Identify the areas in which you wish to disconnect with the controlling perfectionist in your life and those in which you'd like to connect.

*I would like to disconnect from these following areas in which this person tries to control me:*

1. _____

_____

2. _____

_____

3. _____

_____

*I would like to connect, or better connect, with this person in the following areas:*

1. _____

_____

2. _____

_____

3. _____

_____

..................................................................................

As hinted at previously, one of the things that controlling perfectionists want to control is the level of intimacy in relationships. They prefer to keep people at arm's length. You may be used to your suggestions to do things that would bring you and the controlling perfectionist closer together being rebuffed or met with excuses (for example, "I really don't think I can go to the movies with you tonight; I have too much work to do").

An excellent skill to develop in this area is being able to make good "invitations to intimacy" that lead to quality time together. You'll be more successful in this endeavor if you follow a few guiding principles.

First, don't spring anything on the controlling perfectionist, because most likely this person doesn't like having little or no time to prepare. So give some notice.

Second, be sure to invite the controlling perfectionist to do something that you'd both like to do. For example, if your boyfriend hates to shop, don't invite him shopping! If you can't find something that you both like to do, go down to your local bookstore or library together. Just about anything fun has at least one book or magazine dedicated to it. Your first activity together could be finding an activity that you'd both like to do together, whether beekeeping, brewing beer, building gazebos, starting a business, exploring bicycle or jogging trails, doing yoga, playing games, or crafting.

Third, suggest that the controlling perfectionist can do his or her own thing afterward or even before. This is a way to reassure the controlling perfectionist that you aren't trying to seize control of his or her life.

Here are some examples:

- "Hey, I know you've been busy training for your marathon and doing computer research, but we haven't hung out in over a month. I miss you, buddy! So listen. There's an excellent wine-tasting event at the winery on Saturday afternoon. Let's go together. I think they have the wines there that we both like. You have all Saturday morning to work on your computer project, and afterward you can go jogging. What do you think?"

- "The kids are staying over at their grandmother's this Wednesday night. We have the TV all to ourselves, and there's a Matt Damon double feature on. I'll clean the kitchen and make us a nice dinner while you're at the gym. I might even give you a great foot massage. What do you say?"

- "There's a boat show next Sunday morning. Remember how we were talking about possibly buying a sailboat? They have all types there. I think it's free admission. That would give you the whole rest of the weekend to finish your work in the garage."

Finally, don't forget that you have another option: you can join the controlling perfectionist in some of the activities that this person already does. This isn't a perfect solution, but at least you get to spend some time together. If your father watches a lot of baseball, for example, watch a game with him. If your friend is constantly at the gym, maybe you can join her from time to time. Choose an activity that you don't mind or that you've never tried—you might come to like it. Try to keep in mind not to take over the activity or intrude on the controlling perfectionist's freedom, however.

# Perfectionism

From sexual performance, to keeping house, to making home repairs, to throwing birthday parties, controlling perfectionists must excel in all areas. This of course puts great pressure on controlling perfectionists and puts them in an almost constant state of bad humor as they focus all of their energy on whatever task they're trying to do to perfection ("Don't bother me now. Can't you see I'm trying to paint this chair? You made me miss a spot").

Many controlling perfectionists actually dread doing things they insist on controlling, due to the pressure their perfectionism puts on them. Therefore they can also be great procrastinators. Thus, many of their promises may go unfulfilled and many projects may go unfinished. This reluctance to undertake or finish tasks seems a major contradiction to a controlling perfectionist's personality and often baffles loved ones, who wonder, *How can such an energetic, task-oriented person take five years just to wallpaper the bathroom?* or *She's had those copies of her résumé ready for months now; when is she ever going to send them out so she can leave this miserable job she's in?*

Although many controlling perfectionists are actually quite good at what they do, they often make a mistake called *gilding the lily*. Gilding the lily describes when someone tries to improve on (to "gild" means to plate with gold) something that needs no improvement (such as a lily), to destructive effect. Here are some examples:

- "Gosh, the meat was fine the way it was, but I wanted it perfect, and now I've overcooked it. Duh!"

- "So, Robbie, let's go over this one more time. I know I've already said it four times before, but it's important, so you

**127**

need to hear it again...Robbie? Robbie, where are you going?"

- "I couldn't leave well enough alone. The lawn looked beautiful, but no, I had to give it *three* fertilizer treatments. Now it's all burned out!"

Controlling perfectionists agonize over cases like these and live in perpetual doubt as to their abilities to achieve perfection. It's a lifelong struggle for them. But this need for perfectionism can lead to a deeper problem and more significant obstacle in relationships, which we discuss next.

# Identity Issues

As if all this striving for perfectionism weren't bad enough, perfectionism often serves as a substitute for controlling perfectionists' true identity, as discussed in chapter 1. They move away from who they really are and substitute some idealized superperson, setting incredibly high standards that no human being can achieve, "always striving and never arriving." They're never satisfied with anything they do. Because they're always doing what they feel that they *should* do, they end up never doing what they *want* to do. In fact, they usually see their wants as silly, trivial, or unacceptable in some way. For example, a perfectionistic and controlling young woman who really wants to be a nursery school teacher might feel as if that position is beneath her and instead strive to become a college physics teacher. Yet in doing so, she's setting herself up either for failure—because she lacks the aptitude or desire to be a physics teacher—or for spending a great deal of time and energy forcing herself or pretending to like her work.

# Handling Perfectionism and Identity Issues

Believe it or not, you're probably uniquely positioned to help the controlling perfectionist in your life. You can help the controlling perfectionist grow as a human being and begin to let go of perfectionism by helping this person discover what he or she wants. *Really* wants. And that would be a great benefit for the both of you, whether you're friends, family, or romantic partners.

Here's how you might go about it. First, try to take notice of when the controlling perfectionist does something that he or she really enjoys. Perhaps it's roughhousing with the kids or just doodling. Maybe he always watches movies about American history. Perhaps she did something as a child, such as play a musical instrument, that she later had to give up in favor of grown-up responsibilities. Take notice of these things and try to reinforce the behavior when the controlling perfectionist does them or expresses interest in them. Although the controlling perfectionist may not be very good at doing things he or she enjoys, never make fun of him or her for it. Be encouraging. Promote the idea that there's value in simply doing something you love: it reduces stress, is good for your health, and helps you be happier and live longer.

If the controlling perfectionist expresses wants that seem silly to you—for example, he wants to buy a set of matching luggage even though he never travels—bear in mind that this person may be unconsciously hinting at interests. Indulging these wants may lead the way to discovering those interests—perhaps he'd really like to see more of the world. Validate any fantasies, reassuring the controlling perfectionist of the great importance of such dreams.

Use "active listening" techniques (Gordon 1987) when the controlling perfectionist talks about things he or she truly enjoys or gets excited about. For example, nod and express agreement to show that you're listening. Paraphrase back to the controlling perfectionist what he or she has said, to indicate your understanding; or ask for clarification. Be receptive and responsive to ideas and encourage even more sharing. Be nonjudgmental. After a while, the controlling perfectionist will begin to open up more and more.

One of the benefits of helping the controlling perfectionist find "the heart's desire" is that it gives this person a circumscribed arena in which he or she *could* be perfect. The controlling perfectionist may not be able to be perfect in all areas, but perhaps he or she could be perfect in the area of one major interest. While this might not seem at first glance to be any kind of advantage in helping the controlling perfectionist, it is insofar as it limits the area in which the controlling perfectionist could in fact strive for perfection in a realistic manner. Demanding perfection from oneself and others is a losing proposition. Demanding perfection from oneself in a circumscribed area, let's say bowling or playing bridge, is a lot more realistic. Developing deep knowledge or great ability in one area may reduce the need to be perfect in other areas.

> One controlling perfectionist discovered that he liked working in stained glass as a hobby. He did it not as a way to earn extra income or for any reason other than the sheer joy it brought him to look at the beautiful colored glass, work with a soldering iron, and hear the sharp sound of glass being cut. He strove to make more and more complex pieces, concentrating on precision and intricacy. The finished products were beautiful, and all his friends and family raved over the beauty of his creations. This helped him feel adequate and confident in his capabilities in at least one area.

# Stinginess

Controlling perfectionists are notoriously stingy. Many controlling perfectionists like to hang on to what they have—both money and possessions—and in addition are very reluctant to give of any talents or skills they possess or even their spare time. While this might seem like simple selfishness, the truth is that these people are frightened that some catastrophe might strike them and they won't have enough resources to cope. Their stance thus includes, for example, that money spent on having fun is wasted—you should be saving that money to prepare for the worst.

Once you realize that at the core of controlling perfectionists' stinginess is uncertainty of their ability to deal with life's ups and downs, it becomes clear why they worriedly try to manage every aspect of every situation. They're terrified that if they don't control everything, something bad might happen that they're not prepared to handle, showing them to be incapable and thus confirming their fear that they are. Therefore they must always plan far ahead and have well-stocked supplies—money in their bank accounts, tools in their garages, and even plenty of extra food—just in case of emergency.

The fact that controlling perfectionists don't like surprises and will almost always choose security over spontaneity leads to a curious contradiction to the famous tight-fistedness, however: just as they don't want to have to handle sudden bad fortune, neither do they welcome windfalls—whether sudden good fortune or sudden increases of their resources.

> Dennis and Smitty were friends who taught at the same high school. Smitty, a controlling perfectionist, was very fond of 1980s music. So when the student council decided to throw an '80s-themed dance, they approached Smitty. He agreed to take part in the planning and asked his friend Dennis to help him. Part of Smitty's role was to choose the songs that would be played. Smitty agonized over the selection of the songs—he wanted them to be perfect. But the night of the dance, Smitty found that, unbeknownst to him, Dennis had chosen many of the songs to be played that night himself, in an effort to help his friend. Smitty refused to let Dennis play any of his songs, in spite of the fact that he had chosen some very good ones that Smitty had overlooked. Dennis got angrier as the night went on. "Why don't you let me play any of my songs?" he asked. "Because you went behind my back and chose them without my asking you. I'm in charge of this dance, not you," Smitty replied.

The real reason Smitty was upset was that he didn't like surprises, even good ones. He was known to say things like "I love pizza. But if my wife tells me we're having chicken, which I hate, I expect chicken when I get home. Even if she gives me pizza—my favorite—I'm upset. That's just the way I am." He regarded his dislike of such surprises, surprise parties, and so on as only a quirk. He lacked the insight to see that he feared surprises because he always wanted to be prepared for them, not trusting himself to adequately deal with issues without spending considerable time in preparation.

# Handling Stinginess

To begin with, badgering controlling perfectionists to spend money or trying to shame them into doing so (for example, "Our kids are the only kids in the neighborhood who are starting school without new shoes") will be seen as a personal attack and will only harden their defenses.

Instead, address the underlying cause of the need for control and stinginess: the fear of running out of resources and feeling unprepared and unequipped to deal with unexpected problems. For example, you might want to join the controlling perfectionist's strategy of setting aside money for future needs. Several weeks before the school year starts you might say, "You know, school is starting soon and we're going to have to set aside some money for the kids to get new shoes." You might even address the controlling perfectionist's need to avoid unexpected problems by adding something like "The last thing we need is our kids getting blisters and missing school or becoming the laughingstock of the neighborhood. It's certainly good to be prepared."

You might want to consider planning ahead for fun activities and vacations, which controlling perfectionists often deem to constitute frivolous spending. You might say: "I think we're really getting stressed out. We're just working so much, and life is so busy. I have some time off next summer, and I know we'll both need a break then. I think we should start planning early, don't you? We don't need any vacation surprises, right? We'll both end up in the hospital if we don't take a vacation sooner or later." This tactic addresses the controlling perfectionist's desire to (a) plan ahead; (b) acknowledge the level of stress; (c) set aside money for a possible catastrophe; and (d) avoid surprises. You might even want to add that taking a break like a vacation is a good and healthy thing to do and that it's something that normal and happy people and families do. This will address the controlling perfectionist's need to always do the proper thing and keep up appearances.

# Criticism

It almost appears that controlling perfectionists are *addicted* to criticism. Making a criticism, it seems, alleviates controlling perfectionists' anxieties about their own insufficiencies, but only momentarily. Very soon after that, they look to make another criticism, in much the same way that a drug addict would seek another fix. We believe it's as difficult in many cases for controlling perfectionists to control their criticisms as it is for a junkie to kick the habit.

In addition to being a means of controlling others and getting them to attempt to meet perfectionistic standards, constant criticism plays an important role in helping controlling perfectionists avoid intimacy. As mentioned previously, many controlling perfectionists are "intimacy phobic." Criticism pushes people away, creating distance. When a controlling perfectionist feels that you're getting too close, a well-aimed criticism knocks you back a few feet.

# Handling Criticism

A natural response to being criticized is to defend yourself. But remember, controlling perfectionists find it absolutely intolerable to be wrong. So when you defend yourself, a controlling perfectionist will likely respond by strengthening his or her case against you. This makes for a never-ending tug-of-war. If you're not careful in your relationship with a controlling perfectionist, you may become reduced to actually trying to find things to argue about, in the hope of winning an argument for once. The connection between you and the other person weakens as being right becomes more important than being nice to each other or simply being intimate, having fun together, or sharing quality time.

Ironically, people who are critical invite criticism back upon themselves. Rather than defend yourself, you may be tempted to fire off a criticism of your own, as in "What do you mean, *I'm* sloppy? Your car is like a trash can!" Try to resist this urge. It will only result in more bickering, because controlling perfectionists are exquisitely sensitive and overreactive to criticism—they can dish it out, but they can't take it.

Instead, assert yourself. You have the right to be different and to do things your own way. Indeed, you and the controlling perfectionist *are* very different: you have different genes, different personalities, different life stories, different experiences, different ideas, different viewpoints, different priorities, different values, and different wants. Not even identical twins are the same in every regard. People need to do things their own way. What works best for one person will not necessarily work best for another. This, of course, flies in the face of a controlling perfectionist's core belief in a single set of standards for behavior that everyone should adhere to. Be mindful of this and don't get sucked into a debate over whose way is best. Rather, talk about the way that's good for *you*. See chapter 5 whenever a reminder of your rights might be useful or you feel that you need help asserting them.

Use the guidelines for assertive communication in chapter 6. Remember to simply make statements that express your thoughts, feelings, needs, and preferences; don't be aggressive or pushy.

In the following exchange, Paul is responding badly to Evelyn's criticisms.

*Evelyn:* Why do you always scratch your head when you're listening to what I say?

*Paul:* What are you, crazy? That actually bothers you?

*Evelyn:* You're the one who looks crazy; you look like you're on drugs. All you need is some saliva dripping out of your mouth.

*Paul:* *(angrily)* I've never met anyone as critical as you. All you do is nag, nag, nag. Why can't you mind your own business? Here, look *(scratches his head at her with both hands).*

*Evelyn:* You disgust me.

Here's how Paul might assert his rights and use principles of assertive communication in the same situation.

*Evelyn:* Why do you always scratch your head when you're listening to what I say?

*Paul:* Oh, I think it's just a habit I picked up as a kid. I'm sorry that it offended you.

*Evelyn:* Well, you're an adult now, not a kid.

*Paul:* *(matter-of-factly)* I like scratching my head—it helps me concentrate. I guess we just concentrate in different ways.

Note that there's nothing wrong with apologizing for offending a controlling perfectionist, as Paul did. Such an apology can pave the way for mutual understanding. But never feel as though you should apologize for being different. This is *not* the same thing. In fact, when you apologize for causing offense, you're not labeling or saying anything about yourself at all. You're not admitting to being sloppy, lazy, or stupid, buying in to anyone's view that you are, or giving anyone any reason to see you or treat you as if you were.

An apology works particularly well when someone is criticizing you for the tiniest of behaviors, as in the following examples. Controlling perfectionists can be stunningly good at this.

- "Must you point the remote at the TV as if it were some type of gun?"

- "Do you really have to use two towels when you take a shower?"

- "Why do you blink your eyes when someone is talking to you?"

Is it really worth going on the defense over these criticisms? Recognize that some criticisms have more weight than others. When a controlling perfectionist is criticizing you for some insignificant thing, simply say, "Sorry," and forget about it.

Here's another strategy. When you find yourself in a never-ending tug-of-war, "drop the rope" (Greenspon 2001). Let go of the point you were trying to make, let go of trying to feel justified in your views, or let go of trying to get the controlling perfectionist to acknowledge that you're right. Remember, it really doesn't matter if you're right or not; controlling perfectionists will find a way to make you wrong—they *need* to be right, to uphold their self-esteem. So, simply walk away from the struggle. It takes two people to bicker, and once you drop out of the contest, the squabbling ends.

One strategy that many people have found useful involves a process called *reframing*. Reframing is allowing yourself to think differently about something. In this case, consider that every personality trait has both a positive and a negative aspect. You already know that controlling perfectionists see only the positive aspects of their own traits. For example, where you see a controlling perfectionist as cheap, she sees herself as frugal; where you see a controlling perfectionist as intrusive, he sees himself as helpful. If a controlling perfectionist criticizes you for some trait of yours, or makes you feel that you possess some undesirable characteristic, very likely this person is seeing only the negative aspect of the trait. Instead of agreeing that your trait is a flaw that makes you less than perfect (which constant harping may lead you to believe) or arguing that it's not, try reframing your trait in a positive way. For example, if the controlling perfectionist calls you "mushy," point out the benefits of being romantic. You may not at first recognize or be used to looking at the positive aspect of your trait, but figuring out how to reframe your perceived shortcoming may go a long way toward getting the controlling perfectionist off your back about it.

> *Bernard and Clara had been married for twenty years and had two children. Bernard was always criticizing Clara's speech and grammar. He constantly corrected her in public, which resulted in her feeling stupid and never good enough.*
>
> *One day Clara was talking to her girlfriend Anita about the problem. Anita said, "Well, we all know you're not stupid. I always thought that your speech was very creative and colorful and that you spoke from the heart." This stunned Clara somewhat, because she'd really never seen herself that way. As she thought about it more and more, she realized it was true. Clara had reframed the problem in her mind.*
>
> *The next time Bernard criticized her, she said: "I'm sorry you don't approve, but I am a creative and spontaneous person who likes to speak from the heart. I would rather be authentic and real than speak in correct sentences." Not only did this stop Clara from having to defend herself every time she spoke, but it also allowed Bernard to see his wife in a more positive manner, because he valued creativity and authenticity himself.*

Sometimes people have found it helpful to use humor in reframing controlling perfectionists' criticisms; they might see the criticisms as a sign of a stomach ailment, looking at a criticism as a belch or a burp—just some excess gas a controlling perfectionist has to release like so much hot air, making him or her feel a little better. Indeed, there may be some truth to this!

Finally, keep in mind that a criticism is like a phone call. Although the phone might be ringing, you don't have to take the call! If you don't answer a criticism, you rob it of much of its effectiveness.

# Issues of Neatness and Tidiness

Your level of neatness and tidiness (or organization and cleanliness) is a very personal choice. There's no one standard for neatness and tidiness to which everyone must adhere. Even under the cleanest conditions, a person can always be just a little cleaner. But controlling perfectionists believe that their ideas about neatness and tidiness should be universal guidelines.

This can be a very difficult issue to address effectively, because controlling perfectionists can make some very good points about the benefits of being neat and tidy. For example: "Put the cap on more tightly—that way it won't spill"; "Everything needs to be put in its proper place—that way you can find it." Such reasoning can make a good deal of sense.

The problem is not so much that controlling perfectionists value neatness and tidiness but that they take things to extremes (see chapter 1). They make organization and cleanliness one of their highest priorities. They impose their high standards of neatness and tidiness on others, even at the expense of others' feelings. It wouldn't be unusual, for example, for a controlling perfectionist to point out to someone giving him or her a gift that it hadn't been neatly wrapped, without even waiting to see how wonderful and thoughtful the gift was.

Issues of neatness and tidiness are often a reflection of controlling perfectionists' inner struggles. Remember, controlling perfectionists are often conflicted, their genuine desires and emotions clashing with how they think they should feel. They may feel polluted or dirty because they harbor what they view as unacceptable, immoral, or unethical thoughts or wishes. They may feel as if they're cluttered with conflicting emotions. Maintaining a highly neat and tidy living environment becomes a way in which they can feel better about themselves. Using neatness and tidiness in this way, as a means of viewing themselves as possessing a "clean" (honorable, upstanding, etc.) character and thus a measure of their own worth, may lead them to assess others by the same criterion. In other words, they deceive themselves into believing that personal environment must be a reflection of character: someone who's dirty or disorganized or can't seem to uphold the same high levels of neatness and tidiness as the controlling perfectionist must not be as good.

# Handling Issues of Neatness and Tidiness

Bear in mind that controlling perfectionists struggle with internal doubt. Much like criticism, neatness and tidiness is like an addiction, and controlling perfectionists may do everything in their power to continue this practice.

Similar to the way you might handle criticism, point out that matters involving neatness and tidiness are ones of personal preference. It might help if you bring up other ways in which you and the controlling perfectionist differ that aren't contentious issues in your relationship. For example: "I believe that neatness is really a personal preference. It's kind of how you like to sleep ten hours a night and I need only seven hours. That's a big difference between the two of us, yet we seem able to work that out. I'm sure we can also work out these issues of neatness as well." Then stick to your guns. You don't have to defend yourself when accused. Don't let the controlling perfectionist lure you into carping sessions in which you're berated for a lack of hygiene or poor organizational habits.

> *Evelyn:* Oh, great—the magazines are all over the coffee table. It's like a ghetto in here.
>
> *Paul:* I'm sorry the mess upset you. I can put the magazines away if you'd like. I guess neatness is just a personal preference.
>
> *Evelyn:* Come on. Are you trying to convince me that sloppiness is a personal preference?
>
> *Paul:* (*refusing to take the bait*) I think we have different comfort levels regarding neatness.

# A Final Note: Moving from Target to Helper

As someone in a close relationship with a controlling perfectionist, you're in a unique position to help this person if you so choose. This is not a requirement, but an option, something you can do if you feel that you can afford to be generous toward the controlling perfectionist in your life.

One way people develop healthy self-esteem and a sense of self-worth is by feeling loved simply for who they are, usually by their parents. As discussed in chapter 1, controlling perfectionists often missed out on this experience of unconditional love in childhood. While childhood is the optimal time to gain this self-esteem, unconditional love in adulthood can often provide certain experiences that make people feel valued in ways that they should have been in childhood. By consistently loving and accepting the controlling perfectionist *for who this person is* in spite of all the rough edges, you may give the controlling perfectionist a second chance to get a feeling of self-worth and to feel validated as a human being.

Most likely, controlling perfectionists are used to their behavior angering others. They may have experienced contentiousness in many relationships as a result of their perfectionistic and hypercritical nature, with a history of driving away those they care about. This only fuels their anger toward their own imperfections and worsens their insecurities.

Distancing yourself from a controlling perfectionist's shenanigans while still connecting with him or her in important areas shows that you love and accept this person. This serves to validate the controlling perfectionist's true self. When controlling perfectionists find out that their true selves can really be accepted and even loved, they may feel secure enough to begin to let go of their controlling ways.

In this chapter we've covered many issues and strategies. All of this might seem overwhelming. Don't try to implement these strategies all at once. Start slowly. The best thing to do right now would be to go back and pick out some things that struck you as particularly meaningful regarding the controlling perfectionist in your life and then start there. Try one thing at a time. Review this chapter from time to time and then decide what to do next.

In the next chapter we discuss strategies for a very common situation, when a controlling perfectionist is causing you problems at work.

..........................................

# CHAPTER 8

# Handling Controlling Perfectionists in the Workplace

C ontrolling perfectionists are often attracted to occupations in which precision and attention to detail are essential, such as engineering, medicine, accounting, information technology, law, law enforcement, the military, and the physical sciences. Naturally, not all doctors, lawyers, engineers, techies, or accountants are controlling perfectionists, but if you work in one of these areas, or with professionals whose jobs require similar precision and attention to detail, you may be more likely to find yourself dealing with this particular brand of "toxic coworker" (Cavaiola and Lavender 2000).

Here are some common ways a controlling perfectionist may contribute to problems in the workplace. How many of the following describe how the controlling perfectionist treats you (or treats other people with whom you both work)?

1. This person invariably finds something wrong with your work, no matter how well you've done the work.

2. This person expects you to be timely when it comes to deadlines but often drags his or her own feet when it comes to turning work in on time.

3. When this person feels slighted or wronged in some way, he or she is very adept at using passive-aggressive maneuvers to slow down projects.

4. If you're having a problem or something goes wrong in your personal life, this person has difficulty showing any empathy or any type of compassionate response. Instead what you get is someone who wants only the facts (not your feelings), in order to take a problem-solving approach.

5. This person often gets lost in minor details, causing him or her to miss the big picture and thus interfering with task completion.

6. This person's rigid and moralistic thinking gets in the way of finding creative solutions to problems.

7. This person is a workaholic and expects you to make sacrifices in your personal life in order to work just as hard.

8. This person's penny-pinching gets in the way of creatively reinvesting in the organization or leads to other poor management decisions.

## Government Bureaucracy: A Haven for Controlling Perfectionists?

We probably all agree how important government regulations are when it comes to ensuring the safety of the food we eat, the medications we take, the bridges we drive over, and the electrical wiring within our homes. There are myriad federal, state, and local agencies and regulators that administer and enforce the rules and regulations that help keep us safe. However, we're all too familiar with the debacles that occur when government regulators exert their control at the expense of common sense.

On a local level, we knew a café owner who wanted to make use of some shared courtyard space to offer outside seating in the warmer months. The landlord agreed, and the neighboring shop owners were also in favor of the idea, knowing that the café's success would bring more customers to their shops. The township inspector, however, rejected the plan outright, citing some town ordinance pertaining to people eating food outdoors. The café owner eventually moved her business to another town, where she could offer outside seating. The landlord of the old location had trouble renting the vacated space, and eventually the shops failed.

# Six Tips for Survival

So how do you keep your stress level from going through the roof? How do you put up with insults, criticism, and snide remarks that make you want to reach across the controlling perfectionist's desk and strangle this person? How do you bite your tongue when you want to give someone a taste of his or her own medicine? Sounds like a tall order, doesn't it? Here are six key things that you need to remember in order to survive.

1. **Don't show your frustration or anger.** As discussed in earlier chapters, often controlling perfectionists live in a world of facts, not feelings, so expressing your anger or frustration will get you nowhere. Some controlling perfectionists may even take pleasure in getting you riled up, so it's best not to react. Stay cool, calm, and collected, and stick to the facts. This is perhaps the toughest thing on the list.

2. **Don't allow your doubts to override your self-confidence.** By remaining cool in the face of fire or criticism, you portray yourself as someone who's confident, who's centered, and who can rise above petty insults and criticisms. An air of confidence will also help keep you above office politics.

**145**

3. **Respond using assertive communication.** Review the principles of better communication from chapter 6. As an example, let's assume that you've just been criticized in front of your colleagues. Instead of lashing out or becoming defensive, you can make a simple statement: "Oh, I didn't realize the information was not up to date; thanks for the corrections"; "Thanks for the correction—I must have gotten my figures wrong." What you're doing here is modeling an appropriate, mature adult response while indirectly upholding your rights.

4. **Don't expect to be able to please this person.** Never forget that controlling perfectionists are impossible to please, so don't get fooled into thinking that you'll be able to obtain any accolades or praise from this person.

5. **Don't suffer in silence.** One reaction to being bullied is to grin and bear it, in the hope that the bully will soon choose to pick on someone else. Yet if you let someone in the organization know that you're dissatisfied with how you're being treated, this may help you feel supported. Ask that this information be kept confidential, and don't expect that any action will be taken in the short term. However, chances are that others in the organization are also displeased with the controlling perfectionist. If enough people complain, decision makers may take notice, which leads us to our final point.

6. **Don't give up!** If a controlling perfectionist is making your life miserable, chances are this person is making others' lives miserable too. Controlling perfectionists tend to rankle many people sooner or later and to burn bridges, setting the stage for their eventual leaving or being let go. So hang in there. Maintain your focus. Let *others* fuss and fume.

Let's look at some examples of making these survival tips work.

*Stan worked for a large human resources management firm as a talent manager, or headhunter. He'd been with the company for about fifteen years and was regarded as a top performer. Recently, a new vice president, Paula, had been brought in to act as supervisor to Stan and several of his colleagues.*

*What became evident after only a few weeks to not only Stan but also his coworkers was that Paula was a micromanager with a punch-clock mentality. This infuriated Stan, and he began to feel the stress of his interactions with Paula. Over the course of the next few months Stan became so stressed that he nearly quit after an argument with Paula. His blood pressure was through the roof, and his physician told him that if he didn't find a way to manage his stress, he was heading for a stroke or a heart attack.*

*Stan decided to take a couple of weeks off but knew that he'd just be facing the same problems when he returned, so he sought counseling. In his counseling sessions, Stan learned that there was no way to please Paula and that she wasn't going to change. Stan also had to accept that the way he was being treated was unfair but that everyone faces many injustices. As in the well-known Serenity Prayer, Stan learned to try to change injustices when he could but also accept those things he couldn't change. With this new outlook, Stan decided that he'd continue to do the best job he could under the circumstances. Within a year, Paula was offered a severance package after getting into a disagreement with the CEO.*

*Barbara knew from the time she was in high school that she wanted to be an elementary school teacher. She loved kids and loved her many babysitting jobs when she was in middle school and high school. In college she did well in all of her education classes and did such a great job in her student teaching assignment that she was hired as soon as she graduated.*

*Barbara came to her first teaching assignment brimming with new ideas and a passion for teaching. She wanted every one of her students to feel appreciated and to gain a love of learning. In her third-grade classroom Barbara used a lot of positive reinforcement techniques, one of which was "the Goodie Box," a box containing a lot of small, inexpensive toys, games, and puzzles that her students could choose from when they got a good grade on a test. The kids in her class loved the Goodie Box, and it was a good motivator.*

*Then the assistant principal caught wind of what Barbara was doing. The enthusiasm of Barbara's students and the rapport she had with the class irked the assistant principal, who believed that children should learn because they have to, not because they're going to get some kind of reward. The assistant principal decided to put an end to the Goodie Box, using the argument that it contained toys that the children could choke on or otherwise harm themselves with. Because the assistant principal was known to be very difficult to get along with and a tough taskmaster—someone you wouldn't want to make an enemy out of—Barbara didn't let her anger or frustration show. Instead, she tried to calmly argue her point, knowing all along that there was no way of winning the assistant principal over.*

*As it turns out, one of Barbara's students was the daughter of the school board president, and when she told her parents that the Goodie Box was being taken away, the school board president called Barbara, who explained the situation without attacking or demeaning the assistant principal. The next week, Barbara was given approval to bring the Goodie Box back to the classroom as long as some "dangerous" items were removed.*

Both Stan and Barbara were at the mercy of controlling perfectionists, to the point at which their work was being affected and they had become demoralized. As mentioned earlier, controlling perfectionists have a knack for making people miserable and often affect the morale of everyone in the workplace. There were many different strategies that Stan or Barbara could have employed, some more direct and proactive, others less so. Stan was at a point of exasperation and physical collapse, so he needed to make internal changes because there was no way he was going to change Paula or her view of him. So it was incumbent on Stan to change in order to survive, which is basically what he did. Barbara took a more direct approach by trying to defend her position to the assistant principal even though she knew it would fall on deaf ears. She could have told someone else in the administration about her dissatisfaction, but as a new teacher, Barbara knew she was up against a formidable opponent who could sabotage her application for tenure. Yet as is often the case, the controlling perfectionist made many people feel treated unfairly, not just Barbara. One of these people happened to be the daughter of the school board president, so fortunately Barbara didn't have to plead her case further.

Both Stan and Barbara had an overriding goal, which was to outlast the controlling perfectionist and keep their job. What these examples also have in common is that in each one the controlling perfectionist was either a boss or an administrator. But what if the controlling perfectionist causing problems in your workplace is a subordinate or someone who reports to you? You may think, *Just fire the person, right?* However, this isn't as easy as it sounds, as illustrated in the following case. Here the six tips for survival can guide you as well.

> When Alex, a supervisor at a large accounting firm, hired Laura as a contract employee, it seemed like a match made in heaven. Laura had just finished her bachelor's degree and was hoping to begin an MBA program with the eventual goal of taking the CPA exam and starting her own accounting practice. Laura seemed highly motivated and picked up on things quickly. Alex was also very enthusiastic about Laura's ability to work independently.
>
> Soon, however, things began to fall apart. Laura was a workaholic who would spend countless hours at the office and began to snoop around for ways to derail Alex so that she could secure a permanent position in the company. She'd criticize Alex's work to his superiors and make comments when he was even a few minutes late for work, even though he was late only when he took his father to chemotherapy sessions. She began to try to convince the senior partner to bring her on full-time in her own department (which would have been in direct competition with Alex's department) by telling him that she'd do a much better job than Alex was doing.
>
> Alex caught wind of Laura's comments and her meeting with the senior partner through one of the office managers. When Alex first found out, he wanted to fire Laura on the spot, but he didn't want to overreact and have others see him as thin-skinned. He also had no real grounds for firing her, given her exemplary performance,

*and he didn't want to risk a wrongful termination suit. He decided it best to bide his time and wait for the right moment to speak with the senior partner about moving Laura to another office. When he did finally meet with the senior partner, he defended himself against Laura's criticisms and discussed some strategies for how best to move Laura out of the main office or, preferably, how to move her out totally.*

Not only was Laura a workaholic, but also she had incredible hubris (thinking *I can do Alex's job better than he can*), which may be common to some controlling perfectionists. The problem with Laura was that she also wasn't swayed by compassion, which would tell her that it's not right to destroy the career of someone who's been a mentor. Rather than being of help to Alex when taking his father to chemotherapy made him late, she took advantage of the situation. This is a good example of where a controlling perfectionist's rigid view of morality becomes warped. Rather than doing the right thing by supporting her boss, Laura saw Alex's situation as an opportunity to advance her own career. Alex did the right thing by not acting in anger, staying confident, bringing attention to the problem, and defending himself but not to the controlling perfectionist.

In this chapter we'll separately examine strategies for dealing with perfectionistic and controlling administrators or bosses, coworkers, and employees or subordinates.

## Examples from Movies and TV of Controlling Perfectionists in the Workplace

Hollywood has supplied us with some wonderful examples of controlling perfectionists in the workplace. Adaptations of *A Christmas Carol* have made Ebenezer Scrooge, discussed in chapter 1, perhaps the best known, but there are many others.

In the film *The Devil Wears Prada* (2006), Meryl Streep plays the mistress of all controlling perfectionists, Miranda Priestly, who psychologically tortures and verbally abuses all in her path, most notably her intern, played by Anne Hathaway. Indeed, Anne Hathaway's character provides us with some good examples of how to stay grounded and how to stand up to such bosses (although it took her a while to learn how to play the game).

Another excellent example is found in the two *Wall Street* films, most notably the first (1987). In these films no one dares stand up to Michael Douglas's master of controlling perfectionists, the all-powerful Gordon Gekko. Gekko also embodies many narcissistic traits often found among perfectionistic and controlling bosses.

In the TV series *Damages*, Glenn Close is Patty Hewes, an attorney who will stop at nothing to win. Hewes is not only a masterful control freak who has all of her associates quaking in their boots, but also someone who seems to lack any sort of conscience or morals, like a sociopath. After all, the ends justify the means, in Hewes's perverse view of the world.

What all these characters have in common is that they will stop at nothing to attain the perfect deal or to accomplish their goals. Their need for perfection and control becomes their undoing and their eventual downfall.

A funny and less sinister controlling perfectionist is Dwight Schrute, played by Rainn Wilson, in the American TV series *The Office*. Dwight is in constant competition with his coworker Jim to become heir apparent to boss Michael Scott. When Dwight is promoted to assistant manager, his controlling nature goes into overdrive.

# Handling a Perfectionistic and Controlling Administrator or Boss

As mentioned in chapter 1, it's not unusual for controlling perfectionists to be drawn to positions of power. In addition, a controlling perfectionist's preoccupation with rules, regulations, and structure and overemphasis on productivity and efficiency may be seen as desirable traits or strengths, especially in certain occupations. Yet, as we've so often seen, controlling perfectionists often don't work well with others. This is often their downfall.

The importance of working well with others was demonstrated in a landmark study by Robert Kelley and Janet Caplan (1993) in which they studied the differences between average and star performers working in top scientific positions at Bell Labs. One of the characteristics of the star performers was their ability to interact and get along well with others—in other words, their people skills. So it's no wonder that controlling perfectionists can be their own worst enemy when it comes to being flexible and working cooperatively. When it comes to real career advancement, *cooperation*, not control, is the name of the game. Unfortunately, this message is lost on most controlling perfectionists.

Working for a controlling perfectionist is very much a day-to-day struggle. This person may on some days be cordial and friendly and on other days drag you through the mud with one demeaning criticism after another. If your administrator or boss's unpredictability has you feeling like you're on an emotional roller coaster, we recommend that you stay grounded by focusing more on tasks that you need to accomplish than on trying to appease this person.

Below we list some problem behaviors that you may encounter with a perfectionistic and controlling administrator or boss and offer a strategy or strategies to help you deal with each one.

**Problem.** Your administrator or boss is reluctant to entrust you with assignments and tasks, preferring to do everything him or herself.

**Strategies.** Start small. Rather than an entire assignment, request that your administrator or boss give you some specific part of an assignment to work on. This way, you can prove your worth and competence. Here's the trick, though: as you take on this piece of the assignment, check in periodically with your administrator or boss to make sure you're doing the job according to this person's standards. This will hopefully avoid your getting a heaping of criticisms when you turn your work in.

Another strategy is to ask your administrator or boss for some other assignment that you can call your own, on which to prove your competence. If you're assigned a particular task, no matter how menial it may seem, take it on with gusto and enthusiasm and also, as mentioned above, check in to keep your administrator or boss apprised of what you're doing and how you're doing it. Your checking in allows your administrator or boss to maintain a sense of control over the work you're doing, thereby allaying his or her anxieties about the work being done poorly. Therefore, even if you're confident you're doing the delegated task well, make sure to get this person's blessing and input.

**Problem.** Your administrator or boss has difficulty staying focused on the big picture. As a result, you're often left guessing as to what you're supposed to be doing or working on.

**Strategy.** Use the three "C"s of cooperative communication, discussed in chapter 6. First, state your case—for example: "I have about ten things on my to-do list, and I need your help prioritizing them. Can you give me some help with this?" Assuming that your administrator or boss agrees to help you, ask for clarification. "Okay, let me see whether I understand your recommendations. You'd like me to start with the Baker file and get feedback on our proposal—at which point, I'll let you know what the Bakers have to say, and we'll go from there. Then I'm to work on revising the policy and procedure manual, especially the section on deadlines for submitting expense reports. Is that correct?" This allows your administrator or boss to do any fine-tuning. You then agree to commit to the plan and set a target date for when you expect to have the work done and when you'll report back. Although this type of communication may seem like a lot of work, it's better than sitting with your to-do list and scratching your head as to what to do next. This example may not apply to all work settings, but you can use the same basic strategy and adapt it to your work situation.

**Problem.** Your administrator or boss is a workaholic and expects you to show the same excessive devotion to work at the expense of your personal life.

**Strategies.** Be clear with your boss and with yourself about how much work you can realistically accomplish in the space of a day, a week, or a month. It's better to try your best and to keep your own agenda rather than to buy in to an unreasonable expectation set by a controlling perfectionist. By setting your own agenda we're recommending that you take time each day to think about what you need to work on for that particular day. Here, you're defining your daily short-term goals. However, you also need to look at the big picture, so keep track of your long-term goals as well. What goals have you set for yourself for the next six months or for the year? Hopefully, your daily short-term goals will help you achieve your long-term or annual goals. It's important to keep track of these goals, because not only will the controlling perfectionist have you go off on tangential work, but also you may feel at the end of the day or week that you've accomplished very little (which may be a perception your boss shares). This is why you need to keep track of what you're working on, what goals you're working toward, and what you've accomplished. Remember the old adage "Work smarter, not harder," which is essentially what you're doing by keeping focused on your goals and agenda.

It's also important to keep in mind the importance of having balance in your life. When workers fall prey to burnout, it's usually because their work has dominated their daily life to the exclusion of anything that's pleasurable or that serves to buffer stress. So it's important that you stick to your guns when it comes to taking time for your personal life. Visualize telling your administrator or boss that you're not able to stay late because you have a prior appointment. Or visualize telling this person that you're unable to come in this weekend because you're scheduled to attend your niece's birthday party. By setting this type of limit or boundary (see chapter 5) and having planned sound bites of what you might say in this type of situation (see chapter 6), you'll have greater confidence when the time comes that you have to set a limit.

What we often hear from people with a workaholic administrator or boss is "But I feel guilty when I say that I can't stay late or can't work on the weekend, plus I fear I'll be seen as a slacker or not a team player." Guilt is actually a positive emotion. A feeling of guilt tells us when we've done something wrong or have done things that are immoral or unethical. However, guilt can also be self-defeating if you experience guilt in situations in which you have a right to exercise a choice (such as choosing not to stay late, in order to take better care of yourself). You can still maintain the image of being a hard worker and team player by way of your day-to-day work habits. So it's better to be thorough in your work and to make the most of your time while you're on the job than it is to work late or on your scheduled days off. By the way, research indicates that as workers put in more hours or excessive overtime, their productivity and efficiency decrease (see Costa 1999; Kahn 1956; Mizuno and Watanabe 2008; and Wilkinson, Tyler, and Varey 1975). So more isn't always better.

**Problem.** You find yourself getting into heated debates or arguments with your administrator or boss.

**Strategies.** As we mentioned in chapter 6, this type of argument or debate becomes a no-win situation because, even if you're right about a particular point, a controlling perfectionist will often have difficulty letting it go and may bear a grudge. The controlling perfectionist will usually find some way to one-up you, so in the long run it's not worth it. Sure, at times this may mean you need to play the "Emperor's New Clothes" game and agree with things that seem outlandish, but fighting to prove a point may end up costing you in the long run.

Another strategy is to take the high road when you disagree. You can be the one to say, "Okay, I see what you mean, and even though I may not agree, I certainly will consider your point of view." Remember, winning an argument is not as fulfilling in the long run as keeping your job and paycheck.

**Problem.** You're anxious that if you voice any complaint or if you disagree with an idea your administrator or boss comes up with, you'll be perceived as not a team player.

**Strategy.** In most jobs it's important to be seen as a team player. So even though you may be overloaded with work and may be feeling frustrated and angry, it's better that you not voice your complaints or a dissenting opinion in a way that might compromise this view of you. Stephen Viscusi (2008), in *Bulletproof Your Job: 4 Simple Strategies to Ride Out Tough Times and Come Out on Top at Work*, says that it's often better to be the type of employee who's easy to work with than it is to make waves. Just because your administrator or boss is difficult to get along with doesn't mean you have to be difficult to get along with also. So what can you do? Well, consider letting your administrator or boss know something about your personal life or your interests. This recommendation also comes from Viscusi (2008); if your boss knows details about you, you may be less likely to be fired on a whim or for not meeting perfectionistic expectations. However, this is based on the assumption that your boss possesses some degree of compassion.

**Problem.** You like to work independently, but you can't because your administrator or boss is constantly looking over your shoulder and critiquing your work.

**Strategies.** Often controlling perfectionists harbor insecurities and anxieties about their own competence or self-worth, so one strategy is to compliment them or thank them when they've done a favor for you or given you some advice or direction that proved helpful. Although this may sound disingenuous, remember, just as you like to be appreciated for your hard work, so does your administrator or boss. Also remember that your goal is to keep your job, and a compliment or expression of appreciation may go a long way toward creating a better working relationship.

Another strategy to consider when you're being micromanaged is to offer information in the way of verbal or written reports or memos letting your administrator or boss know what you're working on. Make sure that you're specific and to the point. Once the controlling perfectionist feels assured of knowing what you're doing at any given time, he or she may stop breathing down your neck.

## How to Ask a Controlling Perfectionist for a Raise

Even though you feel deserving of a raise, you may find the prospect of confronting your perfectionistic and controlling boss daunting, if not downright intimidating. Use these tips for a smooth and successful process.

1. **Stick to the facts.** Controlling perfectionists live in a world of facts, figures, and precision, so when making your case, stick to what you've accomplished, in precise, clear terms. You may consider writing up a one-page summary of your accomplishments. Remember, your boss thinks he or she works harder than anyone else in the organization, so you need to make a strong case that you've been working just as hard.

2. **Mention how your boss's support and supervision have helped you.** Although this may sound like kissing up, what you're doing is saying to your boss, "If it weren't for you, I wouldn't have been able to accomplish what I've accomplished." This is similar to expressing appreciation, which we mentioned earlier, and you're also conveying that you're a team player in that you're willing to receive and follow direction.

3. **If your boss is reluctant to commit to a definitive answer or amount for your raise, ask him or her to think it over.** It may not be a bad thing to leave the conversation unresolved, because then both you and your boss can think things over a bit. Maybe you can even come up with more and better reasons why you should get a raise.

4. **If your request is denied, ask your boss what you need to do, in a specific time frame, to be eligible for a raise. Write these targets down and then draft a memo that you send to your boss.** Controlling perfectionists often get lost in details and minutiae; what you're doing here is getting your boss to define exactly what he or she expects of you and when you might be looking at a raise.

5. **Refrain from criticisms, negativity, and comparing your salary with others'.** These types of strategies will not serve you well in the long run. Even if a coworker was brought in at a higher salary, this will not help you make your case as to why you feel you're deserving of a raise.

# Handling a Perfectionistic and Controlling Coworker

Working alongside a controlling perfectionist can be either a blessing or a curse, depending on how much this person values getting along with others and being a team player.

Remember from chapter 4, there are things your coworkers really have no control over, and that includes how you behave, your emotions, your work agenda, and your personal life.

We'll now identify some common problems that people encounter with a perfectionistic and controlling coworker and point out some strategies for dealing with these behaviors. As discussed in chapter 2, at first a controlling perfectionist may not want to ruffle a lot of feathers and will try to fit in. However, this person may be extremely nitpicky or point out your mistakes in annoying fashion. What you need to be mindful of is the frequency of this type of nitpicking and whether the controlling perfectionist is doing this only to you or also to others in your work group, because we address these as two different problems. If your coworker seems to specifically target *you* for criticism, this person may see you as a competitor and therefore won't shrink from any opportunity to throw you under the bus in order to make him or herself look good.

**Problem.** Your coworker is constantly trying to one-up you by criticizing your work to others in the organization.

**Strategies.** In instances like this, rather than taking the bait and getting on the same level of one-upmanship, try to maintain collegiality or camaraderie, even when it seems difficult. Keep in mind that you don't want a controlling perfectionist to become your enemy or to target you as a competitor who must be vanquished. We see this type of adversarial situation quite a bit in work groups that have a lot of bright employees who feel that they must constantly compete with one another for their boss's attention. Work groups are naturally more productive when there's cooperation and when each employee is recognized for his or her talents and encouraged to contribute. Think about ways that you might be able to create a more cooperative spirit with your coworker. Is there a project that you can invite this person to collaborate on with you or some way that you can help this person? Maybe you can offer useful information or training. This isn't to suggest that you become subservient to your coworker. Try to develop your working relationship in such a way that you're able to use each other's strengths. Controlling perfectionists are often great at detailed work; you may be better at seeing the big picture—capitalize on these differences through collaboration. If you can't cultivate warm feelings toward your coworker, think of this strategy as in keeping with a famous bit of advice from Don Corleone in *The Godfather*: "Keep your friends close but your enemies closer."

**Problem.** Your coworker's constant nitpicking and criticisms are driving you crazy.

**Strategies.** First, try not to take it personally. You may have to be a little thick-skinned in this regard. Your coworker may be accustomed to merely voicing opinion and have no clue that his or her remarks are hurtful. Remember that controlling perfectionists have a hard time putting themselves in other people's shoes. State your feelings in response to the criticisms assertively (see chapter 6). It may be that your coworker often is critical of you in front of others, such as colleagues or your supervisor. In this case it's best to take your coworker aside to express your feelings, because this sets a good example. It models the way you'd like to be treated—that is, it communicates, "If you have something to say, say it to me in private." It may be good to remind your coworker to concentrate less on your performance and more on his or her own: "You do your job and I'll do mine, and we'll work well together."

**Problem.** Your coworker talks a good game when it comes to projects but often misses deadlines or gets caught up in some minor detail and doesn't finish the job. You may find yourself feeling very frustrated that your coworker can't seem to pull his or her share of the load.

**Strategies.** Remember that controlling perfectionists are often horrible procrastinators and are prone to losing sight of the task at hand. Try to help your coworker stay focused and keep to deadlines by offering suggestions or saying something like "Okay, let's get this report done so we can get it out of the way and move onto other things. Let's set a target date for completion." Be careful, though: just as you don't want to become subservient to your coworker, neither do you want to wind up responsible for this person.

If that strategy doesn't work for you, stay focused on your own tasks and goals. Don't allow your coworker to lead you away from what you're working on. Just because the controlling perfectionist gets mired in minutiae doesn't mean that you have to jump in the swamp too.

# Handling a Perfectionistic and Controlling Employee or Subordinate

Although controlling perfectionists often rise to positions of power or authority, everyone has to start somewhere. Thus in any supervisory position you may have a controlling perfectionist working under you or for you. Here the controlling perfectionist's excessive devotion to work and productivity naturally can be a plus, as it helps set a high standard for other workers; however, there are downsides. For example, these employees often require a great deal of personal supervision in order to keep them on task and to keep their productivity levels consistent. Another downside is that controlling perfectionists often get lost in details or minutiae or even get distracted, undertaking tasks they haven't been assigned in order to fix some imperfection they notice, which diverts their attention from more important or pressing matters. It's as if they have "perfectionistic ADHD."

Some controlling perfectionists also struggle with a lot of inner anger (on one hand they grew up accepting that conformity to rules meant they would receive love or nurturance, yet on the other hand they felt a great deal of anger over feeling forced to accept these rules). As a result, they may demonstrate a lot of passive-aggressive behaviors, which can create a lot of problems for you.

Following are some strategies for helping you manage common problems with a perfectionistic and controlling employee or subordinate.

**Problem.** Your employee or subordinate often shows up late for work, and although this person claims to be working very hard on projects from home, he or she hardly ever turns work in on time.

**Strategies.** Perfectionistic procrastination is not due to laziness or a lack of motivation; it's usually driven by anxieties and apprehensions about doing a job perfectly. You can deal with this by being very specific regarding rules and deadlines: don't assume that your

**161**

employee or subordinate will work independently or will be able to multitask. Also don't assume that this person will anticipate potential problems or roadblocks; instead, have proactive discussions about how certain problems may be handled if they come up during an assignment. One perfectionistic and controlling accountant became totally immobilized in her audit of a corporation when she couldn't gain access to particular documents. Her supervisor simply suggested that she contact a particular person for the documents, after which the audit was easily completed. In your role as supervisor you may need to help the controlling perfectionist plan how to handle any setbacks in order to keep this person on track with task completion.

**Problem.** Your employee or subordinate refuses to keep you abreast of what he or she is working on or give you progress reports. Although you appreciate this person's initiative, you need to stay informed.

**Strategy.** Don't assume that your employee or subordinate is working well on his or her own. Regular updates are important: they'll let you know what's going on, help you redirect the controlling perfectionist's efforts if necessary, and allow you to troubleshoot problems together. Be casual and sensitive when asking for updates, so that the controlling perfectionist doesn't feel singled out or picked on. Try to frame your request as an attempt to help this person maximize his or her potential.

**Problem.** You've tried setting deadlines, but your employee or subordinate still constantly turns in work late because of an overfocus on details.

**Strategies.** First, avoid showing your frustration or making critical remarks. If a project is taking too long, don't let your impatience show. It's better to provide praise for positive work behavior than to castigate your employee for unfinished work or a missed deadline. Try to keep the controlling perfectionist on track and focused.

Second, set clear expectations and boundaries. It's common for controlling perfectionists to overestimate how much they can reasonably do or what they can accomplish in a given time frame. Help your employee or subordinate come to a better understanding of his or her capabilities and limits. Then you can set more realistic deadlines together. Remind the controlling perfectionist that it's not always better to keep working on a project indefinitely: there's a point of diminishing returns where the extra time spent isn't worth it.

**Problem.** Your employee or subordinate believes that he or she can do your job better than you can and seems to be after your job.

**Strategies.** This type of problem was described earlier in this chapter, in the case of Laura and Alex. Some controlling perfectionists get so caught up in being morally righteous or advancing their careers that they think nothing of stepping on the people who may have helped them the most. Here are some strategies to consider.

Establish your authority. In a firm and fair way, make certain that others (including the controlling perfectionist) are aware of the experience and the complex skill set your job requires: there's more to what you do than supervision of staff.

Maintain a noncritical, nonjudgmental approach toward the controlling perfectionist. In supervising a controlling perfectionist, it's important that you provide supportive guidance. If you emphasize that everyone has different work habits and work strategies and that these differences are to be expected, the controlling perfectionist is more likely to perceive your supervision as helpful and useful rather than as intrusive.

Make your superiors aware of the difficulties you're having with this employee. Here, timing is important. Make sure you've gathered enough supporting information or evidence of the problem before approaching your superiors about it; otherwise you may be seen as only crying wolf.

## The Angry Techie: The Customer's Always Wrong

Josh was proud when, shortly after graduating from college, he landed a job in technical support at a large telecommunications corporation. Although he was valued by his fellow team members, when dealing with customers he was often critical and demeaning, and he resisted making any effort to help customers solve their problems in a way that was easy for them to understand. His attitude was "If they're too stupid to understand what I'm saying, then that's their problem, not mine."

As customers began to complain about the lack of helpful technical support, it did become Josh's problem, and he was called on the carpet by the project administrator several times. In these meetings, Josh would become defensive and angry. He was eventually referred to an employee assistance counselor for his anger. Josh felt that the counseling was "a ridiculous waste of time"; however, he revealed that all throughout high school, he had been picked on and bullied for being a geek and a computer nerd. During college he had a few friends, but he didn't date and always felt that women rejected him. Josh was especially angry and demeaning toward the women he interacted with, whether customers or coworkers. Eventually, Josh was let go because of his inability to work cooperatively.

A controlling perfectionist can be detrimental to the smooth flow of the workplace no matter what this person's position is relative to you (administrator or boss, coworker, or employee or subordinate). Controlling perfectionists have a unique ability to put others on edge or on the defensive and in doing so can bring down the morale of everyone in an otherwise healthy workplace. We hope you can use the strategies in this chapter to minimize the frustrations and pitfalls that you may be experiencing in working with a controlling perfectionist. Don't forget, however, that a perfectionistic and controlling boss, coworker, or employee often brings to the table a unique talent for organization and structure. Look for ways to put this talent to best use for you or for your employer.

# CHAPTER 9

.........................................

# Seeking Qualified
# Professional Help

We feel that applying the principles you've learned in this book will significantly improve the quality of your relationship with the controlling perfectionist, providing you're consistent and willing to make small but steady gains. However, in spite of all your efforts, you might still need to seek professional help, particularly if you're dealing with a severe type of controlling perfectionist.

We've tried to cover many possibilities in this book, but everybody's situation is very different. Professional counseling can help you come up with an effective approach tailored to your particular situation, one that takes into account your unique qualities and those of the controlling perfectionist in your life.

Believe it or not, many people are still very self-conscious about seeking psychotherapy. But think about it: If you need help with your taxes, you talk to an accountant; if your car is making a funny noise, you talk to a mechanic; if you need guidance in legal matters, you talk to a lawyer. It just makes good sense to consult with an expert.

# Getting Professional Help for a Controlling Perfectionist

It's not easy to convince controlling perfectionists that they need psychotherapy. As discussed in the introduction, controlling perfectionists tend to see their problematic traits as virtues. For example, controlling perfectionists believe that they're superior to other people and therefore have a duty to correct them. Even when they're miserable, controlling perfectionists have so many blind spots that they really can't see how their misery is the result of their own behavior. They prefer to blame their malcontent on the incompetence of people around them.

Yet in spite of their ignorance that they have issues to resolve and their immense propensity for blaming others for their difficulties, controlling perfectionists will sometimes enter some type of treatment. They might insist, for example, on entering marriage counseling with the belief that they can get their partners to change. Or they may feel that the therapist will pronounce them blameless and psychologically okay. Nevertheless, a skilled therapist will be able to help them see their participation in their interpersonal problems.

## *Talking to a Controlling Perfectionist about Psychotherapy*

When recommending therapy, communicate your care, concern, or love for the controlling perfectionist. Don't bring up therapy during an argument or when you're angry; wait for a calm moment. Also, avoid the temptation to blame. Remember, you're seeking to elicit cooperation, not defensiveness. For example, if you say, "You know, you have significant psychological issues. They were most likely caused by your mother, and you need to take care of them," this is just another form of criticism for the controlling perfectionist. This type of approach won't get you very far. Instead, let the controlling perfectionist know exactly how you feel without making accusations. Be firm.

Try to appeal to the controlling perfectionist's strong sense of reason and responsibility. For example, tell this person that you've noticed that he or she is unhappy and might be able to use some "fine tuning" in his or her life, pointing out that everyone needs help at certain times in their lives. If appropriate, offer to see a therapist together so that you can seek help for your own problems as well. Everyone has problems—you included.

Believe it or not, sometimes a crisis is actually a great time to convince someone that psychotherapy could help. In fact, most people attend psychotherapy as a result of a crisis. Crises tend to break standoffs and stalemates and make people much more willing to change.

A spouse can perhaps put the most pressure on a controlling perfectionist to attend psychotherapy. Some spouses have threatened to divorce or to withhold affection, for example. A romantic partner of any sort is in a great position to negotiate or bargain with a controlling perfectionist (for example, "I won't nag you about your playing basketball Friday nights if you come to marriage counseling sessions with me"). If the controlling perfectionist refuses to attend a joint counseling session, go by yourself. There's still a lot a psychotherapist will be able to help you with.

In other types of relationships with controlling perfectionists, you may or may not be able to use pressure tactics to make them go to psychotherapy. If you're the supervisor or the parent of a controlling perfectionist, you may find that there's some type of leverage you can exert to get this person to agree to psychotherapy. If you have a controlling perfectionist boss, parent, or sibling, on the other hand, you might have to get some help for yourself instead (see "Getting Professional Help for Yourself," below). While this might seem unfair at first—after all, isn't it the controlling perfectionist who has the problem?—you'll find that it just makes good sense. Therapists can teach you new coping skills and find areas in your life that make you vulnerable to perfectionistic and controlling behaviors.

## Choosing a Therapist

If the controlling perfectionist in your life does agree to attend psychotherapy, you may be able to increase his or her chances of success with this treatment if you're able to select or recommend a therapist. Don't simply go by your managed-care health insurance company's recommendations. They tend to refer to everyone on their panels as experts, even if they're not.

Don't be afraid to shop around and ask questions. Beware of charlatans and make sure the therapist you choose is credentialed or licensed in your state. Try to avoid people who refer to themselves as "psychotherapist" or "life coach"—in most states, anyone can use these titles without any training whatsoever. Don't be afraid to call your state's department of health or consumer affairs to ask whether a particular type of therapist is eligible to be licensed.

Most states have associations for specific types of psychotherapists: psychologists, psychiatrists, and licensed clinical social workers (LCSWs) usually belong to a professional association. So if you live in New Jersey, for example, you can contact the New Jersey Psychological Association for a list of licensed psychologists. You might also want to get a recommendation from a trusted doctor or friend.

Be sure to find a therapist who's experienced in working with this type of patient. Ask potential therapists how many controlling perfectionists they've treated in the past or the percentage of time they devote to working with such people. Make sure that the psychotherapist you select or recommend at least has experience in treating personality disorders.

# Types of Therapy

When choosing a psychotherapist—whether for the controlling perfectionist, for yourself, or for both of you—ask potential therapists which theoretical orientation or therapeutic approach they favor. While there are many kinds of psychotherapy, most are at least derived from one of the approaches described below. Research has shown that any of these approaches can be effective when administered by credentialed and experienced professionals (Seligman 1995).

**Psychoanalytic or psychodynamic.** While there are many variations on this approach, these are psychotherapies based on Sigmund Freud's approach. Psychotherapists with this orientation center on their clients' experiences in childhood. They might analyze their clients' defenses and try to bring unconscious and repressed memories to the surface. They claim that their technique gets to the root of the problem. The downside is that this therapy can be lengthy—sometimes taking years—and expensive, and many insurance companies won't cover these types of therapists.

**Humanistic/existential.** Therapists with a humanistic or existential orientation try to create a warm, understanding, and safe place where their clients can explore their true feelings without being ridiculed or criticized. This type of psychotherapy is often termed "nondirective," because the client leads the way: the therapist believes that clients have their own answers and can solve their own problems if only allowed to explore freely. These therapists also try to help clients find their "true selves" and life's meaningfulness to them. People who see this type of therapist often feel especially supported and appreciate the therapist's noncritical, nonconfrontational methods.

**Cognitive behavioral.** Unlike humanistic and existential therapists, cognitive behavioral therapists are very direct and can be very confrontational. Their job for the most part is to constantly challenge irrational ideas involving perfectionism and to help

**169**

their clients reframe their experiences more positively (see chapter 7). Additionally, they might assign their clients homework and activities to do between psychotherapy sessions. By determining very specific goals for treatment, cognitive behavioral therapists help clients quickly address problems, leading to a relatively short time in treatment. Health insurance companies like to use them for this reason. You'll find that there are a good many cognitive behavioral therapists out there.

**Eclectic.** When a psychotherapist describes him or herself as eclectic, it means that this person uses a variety of techniques, depending on the client.

There might be therapists who describe themselves in other ways, using other terms. If a prospective therapist uses terms other than the ones above, do some research to find out what they mean. As a starting place, try PlanetPsych.com (www.planetpsych.com /zTreatment/psychotherapy.htm) or Psych Central (psychcentral .com/therapy.htm).

# The Controlling Perfectionist in Therapy

As a general rule, people with personality disorders are very difficult to treat; rarely is there a cure. However, the silver lining in the dark cloud of controlling perfectionism is that of all the different personality disorders, a controlling perfectionist has one of the best chances of making improvements in psychotherapy. If controlling perfectionists are convinced on some level that they can use some self-improvement, they can be excellent patients, dutifully keeping their appointments and, ironically, trying to be perfect patients.

Under the care of a compassionate and well-trained professional, controlling perfectionists will begin to feel safe to explore the workings behind their perfectionistic, controlling, and critical nature. Getting in touch with their true feelings in a nonjudgmental and professional environment can be very freeing to controlling perfectionists, and they often make significant gains in therapy. Psychotherapy can help controlling perfectionists make meaningful improvements and become better versions of themselves.

## David and Jessica's Story

*David and Jessica met in college. Jessica, a fine arts major, liked to act in plays. David, an engineering student, loved watching her onstage. He was fascinated by her beauty and intellect, as well as her expressiveness. He'd sit in the front row to watch her performances, and he often would attend her rehearsals as well. Even though he turned clumsy in her presence—stumbling over his words and dropping things—she found his awkwardness around her very flattering, and when he asked her out he seemed so smitten that she couldn't refuse him.*

*On their first date David took Jessica to a very expensive restaurant, one that was clearly out of his price range, and arranged to have the strolling violinist play one of the songs from her shows. Jessica was very impressed with David, and they continued to date. Jessica felt loved, cared for, and safe whenever she was around David. He was a wonderful listener who seemed to accept her unconditionally.*

*Immediately after graduation, David got an excellent job with a large communications firm. Being a team player, Jessica quickly adapted to the role of cook and housekeeper while David earned enough money so that she didn't have to work. They were a very popular couple, and they loved to socialize with friends.*

*They had lived together for about two years when Jessica became pregnant. After getting the good news, they married, but soon David began to feel overwhelmed by the impending addition to the family and the responsibilities that went along with it. They began to argue more frequently. Nothing seemed to make David happy. Moreover, when Jessica began to lose her girlish figure in pregnancy, David began to criticize her appearance, her eating habits, and her lack of exercise. At one point he told her that she looked like a cow and that she couldn't possibly turn him on. He constantly compared her to one of his cousins who had managed to keep herself quite slim during her pregnancy. Because Jessica's final trimester was particularly difficult, she needed a good deal of rest. During that period, David criticized her housekeeping and her cooking.*

*After the baby arrived, while they were both happy with their newborn daughter, David's carping on Jessica didn't cease. They quarreled more and more. Jessica tried to defend herself, but David would have none of it: there was no reason for her or the house to look less than perfect. It seemed that the more he criticized her, however, the more depressed and prone to inactivity she became: it was a vicious circle.*

*Hoping to point out how miserable Jessica was making him, David made an appointment with a licensed clinical social worker who had a reputation of being an excellent marriage counselor, a man named Warren Aquino.*

*Through their counseling sessions, David discovered that the pressures involved in raising a child had increased his stress level severely. During one session, David allowed that having a child brought out performance anxiety in him and that he actually felt inadequate to be a good father and provider. Mr. Aquino helped him see that a good deal of his criticism of Jessica was due to his wanting things to go back to the way they were, when he had been more confident. This made a good deal of sense to David, who said that he never liked change because he didn't know how to handle it. He said that he was a guy who didn't like surprises and wanted all his ducks in a row. He recognized that he'd eventually adapt but that he just needed time. He also realized that he was taking all of his stress out on Jessica.*

*Additionally, David discovered that he needed to rely on Jessica more. This was hard for him, because he'd always felt that he needed to be in control. However, he agreed that it was logical for him and Jessica to work together in bringing up their daughter and that it was okay for him not to be a perfect father all the time. Mr. Aquino even helped him clarify his own definition of a good father. Both David and Jessica were somewhat surprised that this definition allowed for him to make an occasional mistake.*

*In spite of David's progress, Jessica was still depressed. She told David and Mr. Aquino that her world had become very small and consisted of just keeping David and their infant daughter happy. She felt that her life had basically come to an end because for the rest of her life she'd be taking care of others. This led to a discussion of what would make her happy. Jessica surprised even herself by saying that she'd been happiest when she was in plays and would like to return to acting. She was also surprised that David agreed. Her theater activities would give him time to bond with their daughter.*

*After several more sessions, both the therapist and the couple agreed that they had the skills necessary to keep them on the path to a good marriage.*

A good deal of David and Jessica's success was based on David's willingness to look at himself and make changes. The willingness to self-examine and to change your own behavior is usually predictive of a successful therapy.

Unfortunately, not all controlling perfectionists are that willing to make changes. In the following story, psychotherapy enabled someone living with a controlling perfectionist to better understand the scope of the situation and, because the controlling perfectionist was totally inflexible, empowered her to leave.

## Deborah and Philip's Story

*Deborah and Philip met when they were in their thirties. Philip, a carpenter, was at first taken by Deborah's childlike charm and close family ties, which he greatly admired because he was an only child. Her warmth and spontaneity were disarming at times: around her, he'd often let down his guard and feel some of the gentler emotions that were rare for him. Deborah, a sixth-grade teacher, was at first attracted to Philip's good looks and high moral values. He was a hard worker and had acquired several houses, which he was working to restore and sell at a profit.*

*The two fell in love. Deborah loved the fact that Philip had fallen so hard for her and was attentive to her every whim. She felt that Philip would make an excellent father someday. Soon they were married.*

*After only a few weeks of marriage, however, things began to turn sour. It was difficult for Deborah to get Philip to take time off, because he worked for a contractor during the week, but on weekends he'd work on his own houses. During his free time he'd read magazines and watch TV shows about home restoration. He couldn't understand why Deborah didn't want to join him in these endeavors, and he told her that a wife should participate in her husband's interests. But Deborah wanted to use their spare time to do other things together, like spend time with her family or travel.*

*Deborah was also upset that Philip wouldn't commingle their finances or give her much money. "We're going to need this money someday, like in case of an emergency," he'd say. He began to criticize her for spending money even on necessities. At one point he told her that the new welcome mat she bought with both their names on it was frivolous and that the old mat would have been just fine. She tried to explain to him how it meant so much to her that they were a couple and how she wanted everyone to know it, but he just didn't understand.*

*When Philip finally came home after a long day's work he'd usually spend forty-five minutes taking a shower, after which he just wanted to go to bed. When Deborah asked him whether he could shorten his showers so that they could spend a little more time together, he replied that he needed that time to get "really clean." Deborah felt that Philip worked too much and she complained that they never had any time together, while Philip accused Deborah of wasting time on things like visiting friends and family. "You only go around once in this world—you have to take every opportunity," he'd say. "Do you want to be a grade school teacher for the rest of your life?" He'd then bring her family into it, criticizing them for not making the most of their talents. He especially picked on her father, who was often unemployed.*

*Deborah felt brokenhearted and deserted. She began to think that she'd made a mistake in marrying Philip. After only six months of marriage, she convinced Philip that they needed counseling. Philip looked forward to having a third party intervene to help him point out Deborah's "defects."*

*Their marriage counselor was Dr. Waters, a licensed psychologist. Both Deborah and Philip liked her: she was warm but very well-spoken and professional. She discussed with them some problems people experience in a marriage in general, such as gender differences, differences in personal values, and how past family patterns can influence a marriage. Dr. Waters validated Deborah's desires to be closer to her husband and to her family, as well as Philip's need to be a good provider. Dr. Waters explained that Deborah and Philip were very good as individuals but needed to work on creating a shared life. She gave them some exercises to practice at home, such as how to ask for things they wanted and how to compromise and, in essence, create a better "we."*

*Problems arose, however, when Deborah and Philip tried to put these exercises into practice. Philip told Deborah that his time at work was "off limits": nonnegotiable. Deborah told him that he needed to pay some attention to his marriage and make some time for working on it. Philip thought it wildly unfair that Deborah wouldn't join him in restoring houses and that she expected him to give up his interests when she wouldn't give up hers.*

*When they returned to counseling, Philip delivered an ultimatum: if Dr. Waters didn't agree that "It's a man's place to support his family in every way he can," he'd leave counseling. Deborah began to cry. Tearfully, she asked Philip to continue with counseling, but he only repeated that his job was his first duty and that his time at work was "nonnegotiable." At that point, Deborah told Philip that it had probably been a mistake for them to get married. Philip said that their relationship was no longer open for discussion. She asked him whether he thought it was okay for her to move out for a while, and he agreed. The next day he called her and asked whether she was divorcing him. He said if she did divorce him, he wouldn't give her one penny or any of the proceeds from the houses. Deborah was shocked that even though their marriage was falling apart, all he could think about was his income.*

# Getting Professional Help for Yourself

Your relationship with the controlling perfectionist has most likely left you frustrated, discouraged, and perhaps even angry. You may be contemplating no longer being a friend to this person, getting a divorce, changing jobs, or even moving out of state just to get away from this person. These are major decisions and should not be made when you're experiencing strong emotions, which will cloud your thinking and judgment. Further, your hurt and anger may make it difficult for you to experience warm feelings toward the controlling perfectionist in your life right now, but if you end the relationship under these circumstances, you may regret it when, after gaining distance, you begin to feel affection for this person again. Under these conditions, it just makes sense to have somebody help you clarify your thinking and feelings. Any psychotherapist will help you make decisions that are truly in your best interest and not based on emotion alone.

Also know that a great many of the people who seek psychotherapy have no psychopathology themselves but, rather, are being affected by someone who does. Most psychotherapists are able to give good advice to people living or working with people who have problems in relationships like controlling perfectionists do.

There are many issues a psychotherapist can help you with. Probably most critical is the fact that you might be complicating some of the issues if you're driven to seek approval, if you need to lean on somebody for guidance consistently, or if somebody in your past was a controlling perfectionist. Exploring and identifying these issues can be very freeing indeed and, a great deal of the time, this in and of itself can be substantial in helping you with your relationship with the controlling perfectionist. You'll probably find that you're doing some unproductive things in your relationship. You may even be contributing in some way to the problems, and a psychotherapist can help you realize and address this.

It's important here to lay the notion of blame to rest. If your behavior is contributing to problems in your relationship, this doesn't mean you're a terrible person. It's usually not even the case that one person is right and the other is wrong; the problem is simply that there's a mismatch between your preferences. If, for example, your spouse likes to be immaculate while you're somewhat messy, there may be a problem, but neither of you is really to blame. The proof is in the idea that if your spouse married another immaculate person there would be no problem (at least in this area), and if you married another messy person there would be no problem either. No two people are a perfect match—there are differences to overcome in any relationship. But sometimes the differences are so extreme that professional help is needed.

If you do seek help for yourself, your therapist will most likely hit on many of the issues discussed in this book and might even use this book as part of your psychotherapy. But psychotherapists are specially trained to explore your deeply personal needs, your psychological defenses, and the many details of your life, something a book can't do.

A psychotherapist will help you explore your limits as far as putting up with perfectionistic and controlling behavior. Some people are incredibly hardy and can let a great deal of criticism and other behavior roll off their backs. Other people are more sensitive. Some people need to feel closer in their relationships than others do. One size does not fit all.

If you do reach a point where you've tried everything—setting boundaries, communicating assertively, exploring your own contributions to the problem, and making numerous changes in your own behavior—and nothing has worked, or you feel that you've had enough, a psychotherapist can help you truly understand the consequences of ending your relationship with the controlling perfectionist. Does it mean a loss of employment? Does it mean financial loss? If you have children together, how will they be affected? What's the true emotional cost? Exploring the costs can help you determine whether it's truly worth it and consider how your life will be different.

Even if you're certain that you want to terminate relations with the controlling perfectionist, psychotherapy will prepare you for healthier relationships in the future. Believe it or not, many people leave a romantic relationship with a controlling perfectionist only to jump into one with another. Other people are left with such a bad taste in their mouths from a relationship with a controlling perfectionist that they jump to the exact opposite type of person, perhaps someone who's too undisciplined and lacks appropriate self-control. A psychotherapist can help you avoid both of these mistakes.

## Deborah and Philip's Story (Continued)

*Philip refused to continue counseling and would no longer discuss the issue. Deborah asked Dr. Waters whether she could help her get through this difficult time, and Dr. Waters agreed that it might be a good idea for them to continue together. She told Deborah that she'd no longer be able to counsel her and Philip as a couple if she were to see Deborah as an individual client. She also told Deborah that she'd need to inform Philip of Deborah's decision and would recommend to Philip another individual therapist if he so desired. Philip dutifully left a message with Dr. Waters that he'd no longer be continuing and that no, he would not seek out individual therapy.*

*Deborah learned in her individual counseling sessions that there was a good chance that Philip would never turn into the person she wanted him to be. She discovered that his rigidity, perfectionism, and controlling nature were very integrated into his entire personality and that change would come very slowly, if it came at all. Deborah recognized that she'd most likely have to give up many things she held dear just to be able to live with him. She realized that this was something she wasn't prepared to do, and she decided at that point to divorce him.*

*Soon after that, Deborah filed for divorce. On Dr. Waters's recommendation, she began to see another therapist for her own individual therapy, in order to discover why she might have been led to marry such a cold man. She began to recognize from these sessions that because she came from a close-knit family, she'd just assumed that she'd have that type of relationship with her husband. She learned that most people who were in her situation would have been fooled by his ardent courtship of her as well. She also learned that when she was a child, her father's frequent layoffs due to cyclical downturns in his chosen profession created a sense of insecurity in her. She learned that she'd felt that by marrying someone who was financially well-off, she might allay these fears. The fact that Philip filled so many of these needs had blinded her to many of his shortcomings. After six months or so of therapy by herself, she felt that she had learned enough about herself in treatment to stop her individual psychotherapy sessions.*

In closing, we hope that you'll keep this book as a reference and continue to apply the concepts we've laid out. As you work on improving your relationship, you'll find that you won't hit home runs every time, but progress will come in small steps and over the long run. Stay firm and committed to the changes you've made in your own behavior. You may be unlikely to change a controlling perfectionist, but you might be able to create an environment in which you can be free to be yourself without concern for criticism or other controlling behaviors.

And maybe, just maybe, the controlling perfectionist in your life will find that a safe enough environment for him or her to be himself or herself as well.

Best wishes on this new venture!

# References

Beck, A. T., and A. Freeman. 1990. *Cognitive Therapy of Personality Disorders*. New York: Guilford Press.

Bernstein, A. J. 2001. *Emotional Vampires: Dealing with People Who Drain You Dry*. New York: McGraw-Hill.

———. 2003. *How to Deal with Emotionally Explosive People*. New York: McGraw-Hill.

Black, J., and G. Enns. 1997. *Better Boundaries: Owning and Treasuring Your Own Life*. Oakland, CA: New Harbinger Publications.

Cavaiola, A., and N. Lavender. 2000. *Toxic Coworkers: How to Deal with Dysfunctional People on the Job*. Oakland, CA: New Harbinger Publications.

———. 2011. *The One-Way Relationship Workbook: Step-by-Step Help for Coping with Narcissists, Egotistical Lovers, Toxic Coworkers & Others Who Are Incredibly Self-Absorbed*. Oakland, CA: New Harbinger Publications.

Costa, G. 1999. "Fatigue and Biological Rhythms." In *Handbook of Aviation Human Factors*, edited by D. J. Garland, J. A. Wise, and N. D. Hopkin. Mahwah, NJ: Lawrence Erlbaum.

Ellis, A. 1979. *Reason and Emotion in Psychotherapy*. Secaucus, NJ: Citadel Press.

Ellis, A., and R. E. Harper. 1984. *A New Guide to Rational Living*. Englewood Cliffs, NJ: Prentice-Hall.

Erikson, E. 1950. *Childhood and Society*. New York: Norton.

Gibbs, N. 2009. "The Growing Backlash against Overparenting." Time .com, November 20. http://www.time.com/time/magazine/article /0,9171,1940697,00.html#ixzz1ZjEyeQeu, accessed October 27, 2011.

Gordon, T. 1987. *Leader Effectiveness Training (L.E.T.).* New York: Putnam Adult.

Greenspon, T. S. 2001. *Freeing Our Families from Perfectionism.* Minneapolis: Free Spirit.

Harris, T. A. 1967. *I'm Okay—You're Okay.* New York: HarperCollins.

Hendrix, H. 1988. *Getting the Love You Want: A Guide for Couples.* New York: Harper & Row.

Honore, P. 2008. *Under Pressure: Rescuing Our Children from the Culture of Hyper-Parenting.* New York: HarperOne.

Horney, K. 1937. *The Neurotic Personality of Our Time.* Oxford, UK: Norton.

Hotchkiss, S. 2002. *Why Is It Always about You? The Seven Deadly Sins of Narcissism.* New York: The Free Press.

Kahn, R. L. 1956. "The Prediction of Productivity." *Journal of Social Issues* 12: 41–49.

Kelley, R., and J. Caplan. 1993. "How Bell Labs Creates Star Performers." *Harvard Business Review* 71: 128–39.

Linehan, M. 1993. *Cognitive Behavioral Treatment of Borderline Personality Disorder.* New York: Guilford Press.

Millon, T., and R. D. Davis. 1996. *Disorders of Personality: DSM-IV and Beyond.* 2nd ed. New York: Wiley-Interscience.

Millon, T., S. Grossman, C. Millon, S. Meagher, and R. Ramnath. 2004. *Personality Disorders in Modern Life.* 2nd ed. New York: Wiley & Sons.

Mizuno, K., and Y. Watanabe. 2008. "Utility of an Advanced Trail Making Test as a Neuropsychological Tool for an Objective Evaluation of Work Efficiency during Mental Fatigue." In *Fatigue Science for Human Health,* edited by Y. Watanabe, B. Evengard, B. H. Natelson, L. A. Jason, and H. Kuratsune. New York: Springer Science and Business Media.

Seligman, M. 1995. "The Effectiveness of Psychotherapy." *American Psychologist* 50: 965–74.

Viscusi, S. 2008. *Bulletproof Your Job: 4 Simple Strategies to Ride Out Tough Times and Come Out on Top at Work.* New York: HarperCollins.

Wilkinson, R. T., P. D. Tyler, and C. A. Varey. 1975. "Duty Hours of Young Hospital Doctors: Effects on the Quality of Work." *Journal of Occupational Psychology* 48: 219–29.

**Neil J. Lavender, PhD**, is professor of psychology at Ocean County College in New Jersey where he also maintains a private practice. He is coauthor of *Toxic Coworkers* and *Impossible to Please*. Neil, who is also an avid blogger, resides in Beachwood, NJ.

**Alan A. Cavaiola, PhD**, is a professor and member of the graduate faculty in the department of psychological counseling at Monmouth University. He is also a licensed psychologist and clinical alcohol and drug counselor.

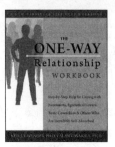

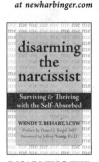